Crafts Across America

More than 40 Crafts that Immigrated to America

By Cindy A. Littlefield • Illustrated by Jim Caputo

JAN   2010

williamsonbooks™

Nashville, Tennessee

ISBN-13: 978-0-8249-6810-6

Published by Williamson Books
An imprint of Ideals Publications
A Guideposts Company
Nashville, Tennessee
www.idealsbooks.com

Printed and bound in the USA

10 9 8 7 6 5 4 3 2 1

Project editor: Patricia A. Pingry
Book designer: Patrick T. McRae

All crafts, diagrams, and photographs by Cindy A. Littlefield, except pages
38, 64, 68, crafts by Jade Littlefield; pages 86, 88, crafts by Kevin Ayer.

Library of Congress Cataloging-in-Publication Data

Littlefield, Cindy A., 1956-
  Crafts Across America / by Cindy A. Littlefield ; illustrated by Jim
Caputo.
    p. cm. -- (Kids can!)
  Includes index.
  ISBN 978-0-8249-6810-6 (softcover : alk. paper)
  1. Handicraft--Juvenile literature. I. Caputo, Jim. II. Title.
  TT160.L56 2008
  745.5--dc22
                            2008009422

To my daughter, Jade, an extraordinary
artist whose creative spirit, refreshing
perspective, and talent continue to
inspire and dazzle me. —C.A.L.

CONTENTS

A Note from The Author

When a traditional craft has been around for a long time, its beginnings can be lost, and we are sometimes surprised when we learn where the craft came from or that it evolved from something quite different. For example, did you know that Hawaiians weren't the first to string flowers into leis? Or that piñatas were originally made out of clay, not papier-mâché? You'll read the history of both of these and many others in the following pages.

In fact, each of the crafts in this book has a fascinating story behind it. And while I include tried-and-true techniques—such as carving, scuplting, weaving, braiding, and sewing—the crafts also lend themselves to new and creative twists.

When making crafts, begin by reading the complete directions and gathering all the things you will need. If the directions call for using the oven, iron, or a sharp tool like a knife or nail, please check with a grownup for help or permission. As you make your crafts, keep in mind that they are meant to inspire you, not rein you in. If you want to create a lampshade collage of flying bats instead of fish, go ahead. The idea is to try your hand at some of America's favorite craft traditions while adding your own creativity.

And above all, have fun!

—C.A.L.

From The Pantry

Unless your cupboards are like Mother Hubbard's, the kitchen is a great place to round up some ingredients for creative fun. Take an apple, for instance. You could cook it in a pie or press it into cider; but for a really unique and lasting treat, carve that apple into a sweet granny-doll face. Tamale wrappers might become a whole family of

Iroquois-style cornhusk dolls, and dried beans could be used to fill Japanese beanbags to juggle.

People from different cultures have used their native foods in all sorts of creative ways. In this chapter you will find a feast of craft ideas from some of these cultures. All will give you plenty of food for thought.

Iroquois Corn Crafts

For almost one thousand years, Native Americans grew corn, which they called maize. The Iroquois used every part of the maize plant. They ate the delicious yellow kernels, and what they didn't eat, they ground into cornmeal and made breads, puddings, and stews. They saved the corncobs and fashioned them into pipes they could smoke. They used the cornstalks for walking sticks. They dried cornhusks and fashioned them into all sorts of things from moccasins to mattresses. And they made cornhusk dolls for their little girls. You can make a cornhusk doll with the directions on page 8.

Can't Face It?

For generations, the Iroquois people have passed down the story of the very first cornhusk doll. Everyone who saw her was amazed at her beauty, and soon the doll became very vain and selfish. One day, when the doll was walking along a creek, she knelt down to admire her reflection in the water. A giant owl swooped down and snatched her reflection out of the water. From that day on, the Iroquois made their cornhusk dolls without faces to remind children to be humble.

Tying an Overhand Knot

This simple, common knot often comes in handy—such as when crafting a wig for a cornhusk doll (step 2, page 8).

1 First make a loop.
2 Then bring one end of the cord under and through the loop (see diagram below).
3 Pull to tighten.

Food for Thought

The Iroquois lived in New York between the Adirondack Mountains and Niagara Falls. They lived in longhouses and farmed the land, growing vegetables, which were their main diet. Their main crops were corn, beans, and squash, and they believed that these were special gifts from the creator. They called these vegetables the three sisters. To show their gratitude to the creator, the Iroquois held a corn-planting ceremony every spring. In late summer, when the corn was ready to eat, they held a green-corn festival.

The Iroquois had other food festivals too. In early spring, when the days turned warm but the nights were still cold, they celebrated the running of the maple sap, which they tapped and boiled into syrup. And in June, after returning from the meadows with their baskets filled with wild strawberries, the people gathered to dance and sing in honor of the strawberry harvest.

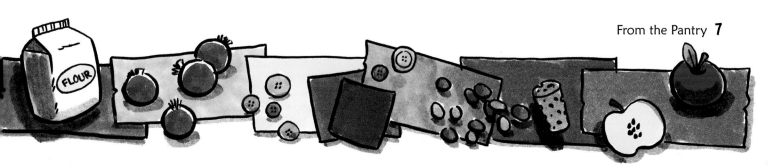

Cornhusk Dolls

You can transform dried cornhusks into a family of dolls. Or skip the shucking and simply buy a package of tamale wrappers at the grocery store.

WHAT YOU NEED

- ❖ **13 tamale wrappers or dried cornhusks**
- ❖ **Large bowl**
- ❖ **Warm water**
- ❖ **16 feet black or gray yarn or string for hair**
- ❖ **Scissors**
- ❖ **Ruler**
- ❖ **Paper towels**
- ❖ **Twine**

WHAT YOU DO

1 Place the tamale wrappers in the bowl. Add enough warm water to cover the wrappers. Set aside to soak for 10 minutes.

2 Fashion hair for each doll by cutting 24 or more 8-inch lengths of yarn or string. Gather the yarn into a bunch and tie an overhand knot at one end. Set aside.

3 Lay 2 thicknesses of paper towels on the counter. Remove the husks to the paper towels. Blot with 2 more paper towels. Trim each husk to about 8 inches long.

4 Sandwich the yarn between several husks and use a piece of twine to tightly tie everything together just below the base of the knot.

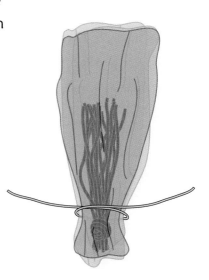

5 Peel the husks down (like a banana) over the twine to uncover the hair. Tightly tie a piece of twine about 1 to 1½ inches below the top to form the head.

6 To make arms, tightly roll 1 husk lengthwise. Repeat with 2 more husks. Tie the 3 tubes together at one end with twine. Braid the tubes. Tightly tie at the end of the braid.

7 Slide the arms between the husks and below the neck. Tie twine around the middle to form the doll's waist.

8 For each leg, braid together 3 husks as you did for the arms. Sandwich the tops of the legs between the husks below the waist. Tie twine tightly around the tops of the legs.

9 If you're making a boy doll, create leggings by wrapping 1 husk around each leg. Tightly tie the top of each legging with twine.

10 Sandwich the doll between 2 or 3 husks, beginning at the waist and covering the head. Tie around the waist then peel down the husk. If you're making a girl doll, leave the skirt long. If making a boy doll, trim the husks halfway between the waist and knees.

11 Crisscross 2 more husks, 1 over each shoulder. Tie both around the waist (see photo).

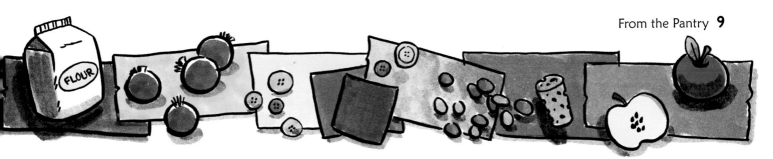

AppaLachian AppLe DoLLs

I bet you have heard the expression "as American as apple pie." But before the 1600s, the only apple that grew in America was the crab apple. It was a lot smaller and more sour than the ones the English settlers remembered from home, so they imported apple trees from England and planted apple orchards.

The apples were eaten, but they were also used to make dolls. Apple-doll making is thought to have originated with the Seneca Indians who lived in what is now New York and Pennsylvania. Eventually, Scots-Irish immigrants adopted this tradition of doll making, and, today, it remains a popular folk art in the Appalachian region.

A BusheL or a Peck?

- Apples can be red, green, or yellow.
- Two pounds of apples make one 9-inch pie.
- There are 2,500 different kinds of apples grown in the U.S.
- If you study apples, you are studying pomology, the science of fruit.
- Ancient Greeks and Romans loved apples. In fact, the apple was their favorite fruit.
- Fresh apples float because they are 25 percent air.
- The heaviest apple weighed three pounds.
- Some apple trees can live more than a century.
- Colonial Americans called the apple "winter banana."

Just Add Lemon

If you want to keep your apple head from browning as it dries, fill a small container halfway with water, then stir in 2 tablespoons of salt and the juice from half a lemon. Soak the apple in the mixture for a few minutes or so before hanging it up to dry.

What a Doll!

Peeling and carving the apple starts the process of a doll's face, but the rest is pretty much up to the apple. It may take a couple of weeks for the apple to dry completely, but once you're looking at your doll, face to face— be it crabby, sweet, or saucy— you'll know it was worth the wait.

Scots-Irish Immigrants

The Scots-Irish originally came from Scotland but had immigrated first to Northern Ireland. The Scots were Protestant, but Northern Ireland was a Catholic country. Even after living in Ireland for close to eighty years, the Scots were still discriminated against. The Irish government closed the Scots' churches, banned the Scots from teaching or being military officers, and declared the Scots' marriages invalid. In the 1700s the Scots came to America looking for a place where they could practice their religion.

Now called Scots-Irish, the Scots came to the Appalachian region that stretched from central Pennsylvania to the Carolinas. They farmed, built homes and communities, and prospered in this new country.

The immigrants remained proud of their Scottish ancestry and continued traditions brought from their homeland. A favorite was to compete in a variety of athletic games, such as wrestling, throwing hammers, and flipping logs that could weigh hundreds of pounds. Many of these Highland games are still held today.

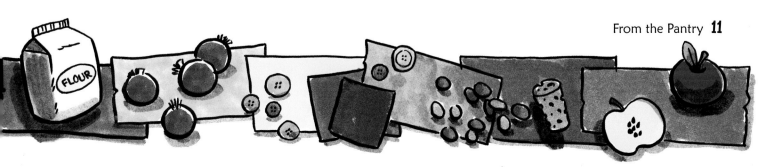

Apple-Head Ladies

The best part about making an apple doll is watching its personality emerge.

- ❖ **Small beads**
- ❖ **Red or pink crayon**
- ❖ **Scissors**
- ❖ **Handful of wool yarn or cotton batting**
- ❖ **Craft glue**
- ❖ **Fabric, 10 x 12½ inches**
- ❖ **Iron**
- ❖ **1 empty 12½-ounce dish detergent bottle, rinsed and dried**
- ❖ **Hammer**
- ❖ **Small nail**
- ❖ **Bottle cork**
- ❖ **Ribbon or lace**
- ❖ **Fabric, 6 x 10 inches**
- ❖ **Safety pin**
- ❖ **Beads and craft wire (optional)**

WHAT YOU NEED

- ❖ **Medium or large firm apple with a stem (Granny Smiths or cortland apples are good)**
- ❖ **Apple peeler**
- ❖ **Plastic knife or butter knife for carving**
- ❖ **Toothpicks**
- ❖ **String**

WHAT YOU DO

1 Peel the apple. Use the tip of the plastic knife or a toothpick to etch a U-shaped nose. Carve away pieces of apple from around the nose, under the cheeks, and where the eyes will be. Make slits for the eyes and mouth.

2 Attach string to the stem and hang the head in a dry place. During the next 2 weeks (longer if it's humid), the apple will dry and become spongy. Shape the face by pinching it or re-cutting the lines. Once the head is the way you want it, insert beads into the eye slits and lightly color the cheeks and lips with crayon.

3 For the doll's hair, you can simply glue some cotton onto the apple. Or make a wig by wrapping yarn around the palm of your hand until you have what looks like enough for your apple head's hair. Slip a single piece of yarn through the top loops and tie it tightly. Cut the loops at the bottom. Glue the wig onto the head.

4 To create a dress, turn under 1/2 inch on one of the long sides of the 10 x 12 1/2-inch piece of fabric and press with the iron to make a hem. If you are not allowed to use the iron, ask a grownup to help. Wrap the dress around the detergent bottle with the hem at the bottom. Tie a string around the bottle to create a waist. Stuff the top 2 inches of fabric into the bottle opening.

5 Use the hammer and nail to make a pair of shallow holes in the wide end of the cork. Insert a toothpick into each hole and very gently (you don't want to break the cork) tap the toothpicks with the hammer to drive them in a bit deeper.

6 With toothpicks facing up, insert the cork into the bottle top. Gently push the apple head down onto the toothpicks. Wrap and tie ribbon or lace around the doll's neck to hide the cork.

7 Wrap the 6 x 10-inch piece of fabric around the doll like a shawl. Fasten it with a decorative pin or bead secured with a safety pin. You can even give your doll a bead necklace or make eyeglasses out of craft wire.

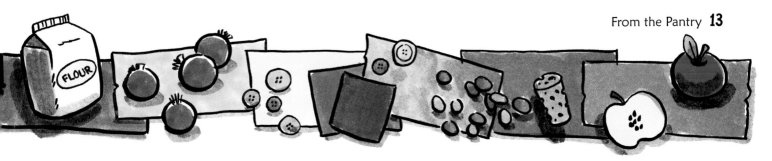

Japanese Juggling

In the early 1900s, more Japanese lived in Hawaii than any other nationality. They had come to the islands to work on the fruit and sugar cane plantations, and many of their Japanese traditions had become part of island life. One of these traditions was a popular girls' juggling game played with several beanbags made from colorful scraps of cloth and called *otedama*.

To play, the player tosses a bag in the air (like tossing the ball up in the game of jacks). Before catching the bag, the player moves a second bag to her other hand (as if it were a jack). During the next toss, the player moves two bags to her other hand, then three bags, and so on. A player might vary the game by wedging the little bean bags between her fingers or balancing them on the back of one hand as she plays.

Japanese Immigrants

When the Japanese came to America, many of them worked at physically demanding jobs. They were often paid lower wages than others, and they were expected to work long hours. Some Americans became resentful of the Japanese immigrants and pushed for anti-Japanese laws that would prevent them from coming to America.

According to an arrangement called the "Gentlemen's Agreement of 1908," the Japanese government set limits on the number of its emigrating citizens, while the United States allowed only those who were joining Japanese family members already living in the U.S. As a result, some women in Japan became what were known as "picture brides" of Japanese men already in the U.S. A man's relatives would send him photographs of a potential bride and, if he approved, the two would marry in Japan by proxy. That means that during the marriage ceremony, someone else would stand in for the groom. The bride could then legally join her husband waiting in America.

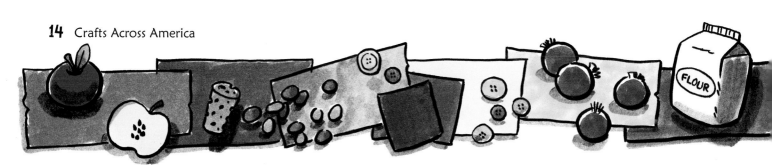

Beanbag Beings

It's all fun and games for this trio of funny-faced characters. But what can you expect from toys that are full of beans?

WHAT YOU NEED

- ❖ **5 x 9-inch felt or fleece**
- ❖ **Chalk or straight pins**
- ❖ **Felt scraps**
- ❖ **Sewing needle and thread**
- ❖ **Buttons and/or googly eyes**
- ❖ **Fabric or tacky glue**
- ❖ **Spring-style clothespins**
- ❖ **Plastic sandwich bag**
- ❖ **Dry beans, rice, or popcorn kernels**
- ❖ **Duct or packing tape**

WHAT YOU DO

1 For each beanbag, fold a felt rectangle in half, matching the shorter edges. Decide where you want the eyes to go and use chalk or pins to mark the spots. You can cut out felt eyelashes, if you want. Glue them in place, then sew on buttons or glue on googly eyes.

2 Trim a scrap of felt to resemble hair. Glue the bottom edge of the hair between the top edges of the beanbag. Pinch the layers together and attach clothespins to hold them in place while the glue dries.

3 Fill the sandwich bag with about ½ cup of beans, rice, or popcorn kernels. Seal the top of the bag with tape.

4 Slip the plastic bag inside the beanbag. Glue the open seams together. Secure them with clothespins until the glue is dry.

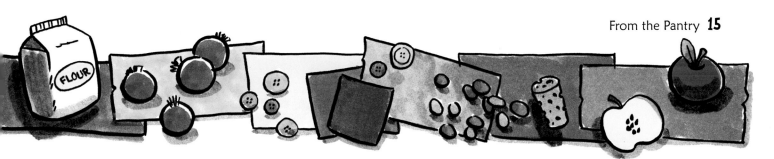

Japanese Ink Prints

Suppose you're fishing and you've just reeled in a great big bass. The fish is so big that you know no one will ever believe you; and the battery on your digital camera needs to be replaced or perhaps you forgot it. What can you do?

More than a century ago, Japanese fishermen learned how to preserve an image of their prize catch. Before they cut the fish up to eat, they brushed it with ink, then pressed or rubbed paper over it to make an impression of the fish. No one could accuse them of telling a fish story! After photography was invented, this form of fish printing, called *gyotaku*, became a Japanese art. Still, it was unheard of in North America until 1952 when a fish scientist named Yoshio Hiyama showed his rubbings to American scientists. The rubbings were accurate, scientific representations of fish. Since then, *gyotaku* has come to be recognized as a fine art.

Fruit and Veggie Stamps

Many fruits and vegetables will produce distinctive prints, as long as they are firm and not juicy. Use this technique to decorate tote bags, dish towels, and place mats.

WHAT YOU DO

1 Cut the fruit or vegetable in half crosswise. Make the cut as even as possible to create a flat printing surface. Blot each half with paper towels to dry.

2 If you're decorating a tote bag, insert a piece of cardboard inside the bag to keep the paint from bleeding through to the bottom layer; otherwise, place cardboard under the item.

3 Pour a different color of paint into each container. Use a paintbrush to apply paint to the surface of the fruit.

4 Firmly press the fruit, without squeezing, onto a newspaper to test how it looks. Experiment with different color combinations and patterns. Once you know what figures and colors you like, print directly onto the tote.

5 Use fabric markers to add outlines, comical features, or lettering to your printed design.

WHAT YOU NEED

- ❖ **Knife**
- ❖ **A fruit or vegetable**
- ❖ **Paper towels**
- ❖ **Cardboard**
- ❖ **Pre-washed cotton tote bag**
- ❖ **Nontoxic fabric paints and paintbrushes**
- ❖ **Small bowls or containers**
- ❖ **Newspaper**
- ❖ **Fabric markers (optional)**

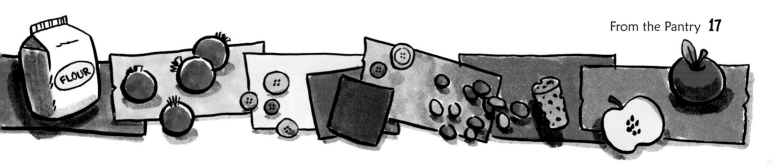

Mexican Radish Art

Food for Thought

It may be hard to see the resemblance, but the radish belongs to the mustard family. It traces its history back to ancient China, but this peppery-tasting root vegetable made an early appearance in the Americas. In the 1500s the Spanish colonists brought radishes to Mexico and planted them. Were they in for a surprise! The radishes thrived in the rich, stony soil and grew as big as potatoes.

The radishes' knobby shapes inspired Mexican artists to sculpt them into all sorts of figures and creatures. Before long, carving radishes was a popular Christmastime tradition. Still today, every December 23, the town of Oaxaca hosts *Noche de los Rabanos*, which means "Night of the Radish." Thousands of people come to see the elaborate radish displays. Popular scenes include the Nativity and other Bible stories and significant moments in Mexico's history.

Unlike radishes grown in Mexico, those grown in the U.S. are typically small, round, and smooth. Their ball-like shape has inspired many chefs to carve them into a bouquet of roses to use as a table centerpiece.

Carved Clay Bouquet

Instead of carving real radishes, round up a bunch out of clay to carve into flowers that will last forever.

WHAT YOU NEED

- **White and red polymer clay (such as Fimo or Sculpey)**
- **Wax paper**
- **Rolling pin**
- **Plastic knife or butter knife**
- **Bamboo kitchen skewers**
- **Foil**
- **Cookie sheet**
- **Green permanent marker**
- **Tacky glue**

WHAT YOU DO

1 Preheat the oven to 275°F or the temperature on the clay package directions.

2 Knead each batch of clay to soften it. For each rose you are making, shape a 1-inch ball of white clay and set aside. (Use about ¼ of the package.)

3 Place a marble-sized ball of red clay between 2 sheets of wax paper and roll it out to a ⅛-inch thickness. Roll out a thin sheet of red clay for each rose.

4 Wrap the red clay around each white clay ball, smoothing seams.

5 Working with one ball at a time, slice a thin piece off the top. Slice partway down through the clay. Repeat 3 times to create 4 outer petals. Gently pinch each petal and pull the top away from the center. Repeat slicing and pulling to create an inner round of petals.

7 Poke a stem hole in the bottom of each rose with the point of a kitchen skewer. Carefully set the flowers on their base on a foil-covered cookie sheet.

8 Bake the roses according to the clay package directions. When the baking time is up, use oven mitts to remove the cookie sheet and place it on a wire rack. Cool thoroughly before touching.

9 Use the green marker to color a bamboo skewer for each rose. When the flowers have cooled, fit the roses onto bamboo stems (see photo). Use a bit of glue to hold them.

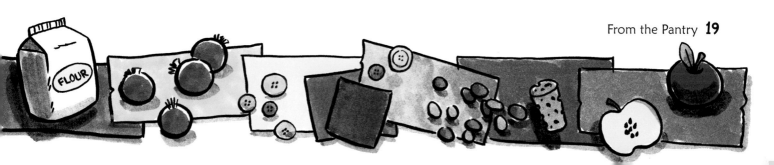

German Doughcraft

Salt dough is the perfect texture—soft and squishy—for rounding up a flock of billowy sheep. To add variety, you can tint a portion of the dough with cocoa.

WHAT YOU NEED

- ❖ **Straight-style clothespins, 2 per sheep**
- ❖ **Brown craft paint**
- ❖ **Paintbrush**
- ❖ **Large bowl**
- ❖ **1 cup flour, plus additional**
- ❖ **1 cup salt**
- ❖ **½ cup water**
- ❖ **Wooden spoon**
- ❖ **Wax paper**
- ❖ **Cocoa**
- ❖ **Small beads**
- ❖ **Craft glue**
- ❖ **Sandpaper**

WHAT YOU DO

1 Paint the clothespins brown and set them aside to dry.

2 In the large bowl, combine flour, salt, and water. Stir with a wooden spoon, mixing well. Lay a large piece of wax paper on the counter; lightly sprinkle it with flour. Turn out dough onto the floured wax paper and knead until the dough is smooth.

3 Pull off ¼ of the dough; knead some cocoa into it to turn it a nice brown. Set aside.

4 For each sheep, shape a small plum-sized piece of white dough into a body-shaped lump.

5 Push the tops of two clothespins into the bottom of the body for legs.

6 From a small piece of cocoa dough, mold an oval face.

7 With another piece of cocoa dough, mold a short, thick rope for a set of ears. Gently press them in place on the head and then press the head onto the body.

8 Carefully place one sheep on a microwave-safe plate. Microwave sheep for 10 seconds. Turn sheep over and microwave another 10 seconds. (Turning keeps the sheep from becoming flat on one side.) Repeat until the dough is fairly firm. *Caution: the dough will be hot. Let it cool each time before touching it.*

9 When the sheep is completely cool, glue on beads for eyes.

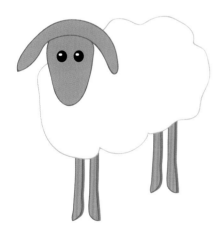

10 Finally, see if each sheep can stand on its own. If not, lightly sand the bottoms of the clothespin legs to level them.

Here's The Story

Doughcraft, the art of molding decorations out of a mixture of flour, salt, and water, comes from old-world Germany. It was particularly popular in the 1800s, when poor farming families used it to make Christmas tree ornaments. They added extra salt to the dough to discourage mice from eating them. Salt dough was also a traditional gift for German newlyweds. Presented by the mother of the bride, it was meant to bring good luck to the new couple.

When the Germans immigrated to the U.S., they settled in Pennsylvania, along the Appalachians, and later in the upper midwestern states of Wisconsin, Ohio, and Minnesota where they developed large farms. The Germans were outstanding farmers and carefully cleared the land and built huge barns for their animals. They built covered wagons to deliver their crops to market. These were the Conestoga wagons, named after a creek in Pennsylvania and later used by pioneers heading west.

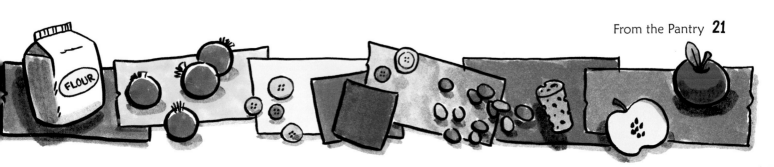

Sticks To Stones

Packing up all of your family's belongings and moving from your homeland to a country you have never seen before is no easy decision! What swayed thousands upon thousands of immigrants from around the world to settle in America during her early days as a nation? For many it was the opportunity to practice religious freedom, but the quest for land was attractive too.

For a time, people could acquire land in America simply by settling on it. That didn't mean life was easygoing. Living in the mountains, plains, and deserts alike posed its challenges. Still, each of these regions also offered unique rewards, and it wouldn't be long before the settlers were using the natural resources they found in their new environments in creative ways. Let's take a look at a few of these creative crafts.

RATTLE RATTLE

Celtic Tree of Life

In many ancient cultures, the tree represented the connection between heaven and earth, with its branches stretching skyward and its roots reaching down into the ground. For instance, when a child was born to an Irish, Scot, or other Celtic family, they would plant a tree. The family hoped this tree would allow the child's imagination to flourish, just as a tree continues to grow its whole life.

Twisted Wire Tree

Using a stone for a base and craft wire for the trunk and branches, sculpt a miniature tree of life to decorate your dresser top or a desk. Not only will it make an interesting conversation piece, it also will serve as a reminder that when it comes to creating arts and crafts, the sky's the limit!

WHAT YOU NEED

* **Flexible craft wire**
* **Wire cutters**
* **A stone**
* **Green leaf-shaped sequins**
* **Polymer clay**
* **Toothpick**
* **String**

WHAT YOU DO

1 Cut at least twenty 36-inch lengths of wire. Divide wire pieces into two bundles. Twist the center of each bundle several times to hold the wires together.

2 Lay 1 bundle of wire on top of the other to form an X and set your stone in the middle of the bundle.

3 Bend the wires up around the sides of the stone and, holding them together with one hand, twist repeatedly to form a tree trunk about 4 inches tall.

4 To form branches, separate the wires above the trunk into 4 groups. Twist each group until the twisted portion is 2 or 3 inches long. Separate the wires into 2 groups and twist them a few inches more. Repeat this process until you reach the ends of the branches.

5 For leaves, slide sequins onto the wire tips.

6 Shape a swing seat out of polymer clay. Use a toothpick to poke a hole through each side.

7 Bake the clay according to the package directions and let it cool.

8 Cut 2 pieces of string, each 4 inches long. Thread string through the hole and knot the end under the seat. Repeat for other side of seat.

9 Tie both loose ends of the string to one of the tree limbs.

Knock on Wood

The ancient Celts believed that spirits lived in trees. As a result, they started the "knock on wood" custom. When a person boasts about something—that they've never had a toothache, for example—they will quickly knock on a piece of wood. The old Irish belief is that touching or knocking on a tree is a way to thank the leprechauns for good luck.

Irish Immigrants

The Celtic Irish came to America in the 1800s during a time when 80 percent of Ireland was rural and much of it had been used to grow potatoes. When the potato blight destroyed Ireland's crop in 1845, it caused a devastating famine. As a result, about one-third of Ireland's population left.

These Irish immigrants introduced two holiday traditions to the United States that are still popular today. One, of course, is Saint Patrick's Day; the other is Halloween. In ancient times, October 31 was considered the last day of the old year, and many people thought restless spirits came out that night to roam the land and destroy the crops. To deter them, the Irish farmers would light lanterns made from turnips that had been carved to resemble scary faces. When Irish immigrants came to America, they discovered that the native pumpkins were much easier to sculpt, and a new generation of jack-o'-lanterns was born.

Animalitos

In the tiny villages surrounding the city of Oaxaca, Mexico, the farmers grow corn and beans just like their ancestors did for hundreds of years. But in the past few decades, many of them began a second occupation carving distinctive wooden *animalitos*—frogs, dogs, lizards, and all kinds of other critters. Exactly which creature the artist will choose to carve is often inspired by the shape of or a twist in the piece of wood. Even before they're painted, animalitos often look animated, but it's their brilliant colors and fanciful patterns of dots, spots, and lines that really bring them to life. Animalitos have traveled far from their Mexican roots, gaining popularity with folk art collectors in America—and bringing good fortune to the farmers who whittle them. An early collector was Nelson Rockefeller, a former Vice President of the United States, who discovered Oaxacan artwork while visiting Mexico in the 1960s and brought some pieces home with him. By the mid-1980s, these brightly painted carvings could be found on gift shop shelves across America as well as Europe.

Wooden Spool Snake

With this corn snake animalito, the wood is already carved and ready to paint. To make it, you simply string wooden thread spools into a slithery snake. A bold spattering of dots, much like the patterns used to decorate Oaxacan woodcarvings, give it its colorful scales.

WHAT YOU NEED

- ❖ **Wooden thread spools as below:**
  16 3/4-inch spools
  2 5/8-inch spools
  2 3/8-inch spools
  2 1/2-inch spools
- ❖ **Yellow, red, and black acrylic paints**
- ❖ **Paintbrush**
- ❖ **Cotton swabs**
- ❖ **At least 24 inches thin red cord or elastic**

WHAT YOU DO

1 Paint all of the thread spools yellow. Set them aside to dry.

2 Dip the end of a cotton swab into red paint. Apply a large patch of red dots on each spool. Paint dots for eyes on the sides of one larger spool for the snake's head.

3 Dip a clean cotton swab into black paint and dab a ring of black dots around each of the red patches. Paint black pupils in the eyes.

4 Allow the paint to completely dry. Line up the spools from smallest to largest. Knot one end of the cord or elastic. Begin with the smallest spools and thread the cord through each spool, working from the smallest up to the larger ones.

5 Tie another knot as close to the head spool as possible. Cut the cord an inch or so beyond the knot for the snake's tongue.

Chilean Rainmakers

The Atacama Desert of northern Chile in South America is sandwiched between the Pacific Ocean and the Andes Mountains and is one of the driest places on earth. In some parts of the desert, rain has never been recorded. No wonder the Diguita farmers who live in the region tried to boost the odds of a downpour by serenading the gods with rainsticks.

To make their sticks, the Diguita cut off dead cactus branches and pressed their thorny spines into the hollowed centers. Then they filled the branches with pebbles collected from the desert.

Here's The Story

It's not certain where the Diguita came up with the idea of a rainstick. Some people say it may have been from Africans who traveled through South America in the early 1500s. That's because Diguita rainsticks resemble a tube-shaped rattle that is common in west Africa. These days, the Chilean rainstick is more often used to serenade audiences far from the Atacama Desert; it's become a popular instrument with musicians around the world, including those in the United States. You can also find rainsticks in gift shops all across the country.

RaTTLing RainStick

You don't need a spiny cactus to make a rainstick. A mailing tube and nails will work just fine. And rather than filling it with pebbles, experiment with dried beans, peas, or rice, and pick your favorite sound.

WHAT YOU NEED

* **Hammer**
* **48 3- or 4-penny nails for a 1½ x 24-inch tube *or* 96 8-penny nails for a 3 x 24-inch tube**
* **Mailing tube with caps for the ends**
* **Newspaper**
* **Masking tape**
* **Scissors**
* **Measuring tape**
* **Decorative wrapping paper**
* **Double-sided tape**
* **1 cup dried beans, peas, lentils, or rice**

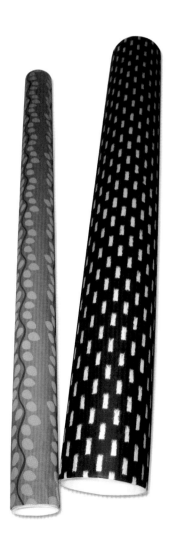

WHAT YOU DO

1 Randomly hammer all of the nails into the mailing tube to create an inner grid for the beans to fall through.

2 Cover the nails by wrapping newspaper around the tube and using masking tape to hold it in place.

3 Cut a piece of decorative paper that is as long as the tube and as wide as the tube's circumference plus 1 inch. Place the paper, printed side down, on a table and apply strips of double-sided tape along all 4 edges.

4 Set the tube on one of the paper's long edges. Slowly roll the tube to wrap it, pressing down on the taped portions and smoothing the paper as you go.

5 Place one of the caps on the tube. Pour the beans, peas, lentils, or rice into the other end. Place the cap on tight. Slowly tilt the tube upright and listen to the beans spill through the grid. You can add or remove some beans or replace them with other types of seeds to compare the sounds.

Swedish Ornaments

Pretend you're living in Sweden. It's Christmas night, and, all of a sudden, you hear a loud thump at the door. When you go outside to see what it is, you discover an ornament fashioned out of straw tied with thread. A little ram, perhaps, or maybe a pretty star. Throwing ornamental straw figures *(julshomme)* has long been a popular Swedish tradition and one that continued with Swedish families who moved to America. During the late nineteenth century through the beginning of the twentieth century, more than a million Swedes immigrated to America—nearly a quarter of Sweden's population at the time. Many of these families were drawn to the upper Midwest where, thanks to President Lincoln's Homestead Act, they could claim land to farm.

Food for Thought

Have you ever been to a smorgasbord? This help-yourself-style meal has long been popular among America's Swedish immigrants, particularly during the holiday season. A traditional spread includes ham, Swedish meatballs, dilled potatoes, roasted beets, fruit soup, and gingersnaps, which the Swedes sometimes call Pepper Cookies.

So What's The Homestead Act?

The Homestead Act, which became law on January 1, 1863, allowed anyone to file for a quarter-section (160 acres) of free land. At the end of five years, the land was deeded to the settler if he had built a house, dug a well, plowed ten acres, built a fence, and actually lived on the land.

Fuzzy Snowflake

Here's how you can add a colorful twist to traditional Swedish star ornaments.
Instead of using straw and thread, gather a handful of pipe cleaners and pony beads.

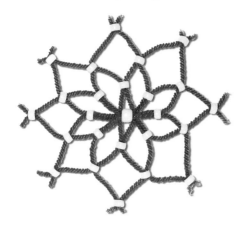

WHAT YOU NEED

* ❖ **Pipe cleaners**
* ❖ **Scissors or wire cutters**
* ❖ **Pony beads, some large and some small**

WHAT YOU DO

1 Cut eight 6-inch lengths of pipe cleaners. Lay them straight and together. Thread all 8 pipe cleaners through a large pony bead.

2 Slide the bead to the middle of the bunch. Fan out the pipe cleaner ends.

3 Starting on the left, pair 1 pipe cleaner end from above the bead with another from below it. Slide a small pony bead onto the pair, positioning it about ½ inch from the center bead. Work your way around the star, pairing up the pipe cleaner ends this way.

4 For the second round, pair together pipe cleaner ends from neighboring beads and slide on beads, positioning them about an inch from the end.

5 Again, pair together pipe cleaner ends from neighboring beads and slide on another round of beads. Spread the pipe cleaner tips slightly to keep the beads from falling off.

Six-Point Star

WHAT YOU NEED

❖ **Pipe cleaners**

❖ **Scissors or wire cutters**

❖ **Pony beads, large and small**

WHAT YOU DO

1 Cut nine 6-inch lengths of pipe cleaners. Lay them straight and together. Thread all 9 pipe cleaners through a large pony bead.

2 Slide the bead to the middle of the bunch. Fan out the pipe cleaner ends.

3 Starting on the left, pair up one pipe cleaner end from above the bead with another from below it. Slide the ends through a small pony bead and position it about ½ inch from the center bead. Skip a pipe cleaner and pair up the next two pipe cleaners. Slide on a small pony bead. Work your way around the star, pairing up pipe cleaner ends this way.

4 For the second round, pair up each single pipe cleaner you skipped last time with the pipe cleaners on either side of it. Push the 3 ends through 2 small pony beads as in the photo.

5 Spread the pipe cleaner tips slightly to keep the beads from falling off.

Square Inside a Star

WHAT YOU NEED

- **Pipe cleaners**
- **Scissors or wire cutters**
- **Pony beads, large and small**

WHAT YOU DO

1 Gather eight 6-inch pipe cleaner lengths into a bunch, then push the ends through a large pony bead. Slide it to the center.

2 Pull together 2 pipe cleaner ends from above the bead and 2 from below it and push all 4 ends through a large bead, stopping ½ inch

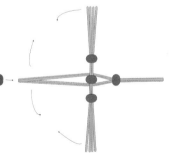

from the center bead. Work your way around the star, creating 3 more groups of 4 pipe cleaners.

3 Pair up a pipe cleaner end from 1 group with 1 from another group. Slide on a 2 small pony beads, and spread the ends to keep the beads in place. Work your way around the star, pairing up the remaining ends as shown.

4 Spread the pipe cleaner tips slightly to keep the beads from falling off.

Navajo Sand Art

Sand painting was an important part of the ceremonies that the Navajo medicine men performed to cure the sick. These paintings were usually created right on the floor of the family's hut. At the end of the ceremony, the sand was swept up and buried or scattered. This style of sand painting is still done today, often as part of a ceremony to honor the birth of a child, a marriage, a new home, or even a job. For these occasions, the sand paintings are smaller and typically created on a piece of buckskin or cloth.

In recent times, Navajo artists developed a more permanent variation of sand painting in which they sprinkle finely crushed stone onto the glued surface of plywood boards. To show respect for the difference between these pictures and ceremonial paintings, the artists are careful not to create exact copies of traditional designs.

The Pueblo Indians

In the late 1600s, when the Spanish came to the region that is now El Paso, Texas, many of the Pueblo people living there fled and resettled among the Navajos in what is now New Mexico and Arizona. The Pueblos continued their own customs and even taught them to the Navajos. These traditional crafts included weaving and painting with colored sand, crushed rock, and cornmeal.

Sandpaper Paintings

Sandpaper makes a great canvas for sand painting. It's lightweight yet sturdy. It also saves you from having to fill in the background, so you can start right in coloring your design.

WHAT YOU NEED

- ❖ **Scissors**
- ❖ **Fine (150 gauge) sandpaper**
- ❖ **Pencil**
- ❖ **Colored sand**
- ❖ **White glue**
- ❖ **Small paintbrush**
- ❖ **Tray or box for catching loose sand**
- ❖ **Double-sided tape (optional)**
- ❖ **Colored paper (optional)**

WHAT YOU DO

1 Cut a piece of sandpaper to the size you like (those shown here are ¼ of a sheet). Lightly sketch your design on it. (You may want to practice on scrap paper first.) You can trace around a picture cut from a magazine or coloring book, if you wish.

2 Choose the color sand you want to start with and paint the corresponding portions of your design with glue. It's a good idea to save white or very light colors for last.

3 Sprinkle sand over the glue (keep in mind that a little goes a long way).

4 Hold the sandpaper over the tray or box and tap the back to knock off any loose sand. After each color, return the loose unused sand to the new so you can reuse it.

5 Once your painting is finished, you can accent your artwork with a colorful paper frame. Attach strips of double-sided tape to the back of the sandpaper and press your painting onto a slightly larger sheet of colored paper.

Native American Pinch Pots

For thousands of years before European settlers brought metal kettles to North America, the native tribes living in the New England area made pots of clay dug from seaside cliffs and from the banks of ponds and rivers. So the clay could withstand the heat of the coals, the Native Americans mixed sand, crushed shells, or dried plants into it. After they had shaped the pot, they often pressed the rippled surface of a shell or the end of a stick into the clay to create a pattern of lines.

Some pots were made with pointed bottoms that could be wedged down into the hot coals for faster and hotter cooking. Other pots had narrow necks designed for hanging above a fire for slower cooking. After the pots were fired, they were rock-hard and ready to cook and store food.

Food for Thought

When the English first settled in America, Native Americans taught them how to prepare baked beans. They dug a hole in the ground, lined it with hot stones, and then set in the pot. The natives flavored their beans with maple syrup and bear fat. The colonists substituted molasses and salt pork.

Baked beans became a favorite dish for Sunday dinner. On Saturday the women set their bean pots in their brick ovens to cook overnight and be ready the next day. In this way they avoided working on the Sabbath.

CoiLed CLay BowLS

By using air-drying clay, you can shape a whole collection of Native American style pots and decorate them with stamped patterns and colorful beads and stones. The best part is you won't have to "fire" your pots because they'll harden on their own.

WHAT YOU NEED

- ❖ **Newspapers**
- ❖ **Wax paper**
- ❖ **Air-drying terra-cotta colored clay**
- ❖ **Wooden spoon**
- ❖ **Plastic fork or hair comb**
- ❖ **Beads or buttons**
- ❖ **Wire baking rack**

WHAT YOU DO

1 Spread newspapers over your work surface. Over the newspapers, lay down a large sheet of wax paper.

2 Tear off a golf-ball size piece of clay and roll it into a ball. Press it flat, about ¼ inch thick. This is the base for your pot.

3 Roll more of the clay between your palms to form a long rope and coil it on top of the base to form the sides of the pot. Repeat this step until the pot is the size you like.

4 Using your fingers or the back of a wooden spoon, smooth the coils until the clay is seamless inside and out. Don't rush this step. It is very important to blend the coils or they may pull apart as the clay dries. For the best results, try not to press the clay too thin.

5 Decorate the outside of the pot by using the prongs of a plastic fork to make a pattern. Or create lines by pressing the teeth of the comb against the pot. You can also push beads or buttons partway into the clay. Smooth a bit of clay over the edges of the buttons to keep them from popping off when the pot dries.

6 Set the completed pots on the wire rack to dry. Check the pots each day for a few days. If you notice the clay cracking in spots, moisten a bit of new clay with a few drops of water and smooth it into and over the gaps.

Stacked Stones

Here's an optical illusion you can call well-done: one scrumptious-looking burger with pickles on the side. The trick? There's no beef. In fact, this whole meal—sesame-seed bun and all—is made of stones.

WHAT YOU NEED

- ❖ **Small rocks or stones**
- ❖ **Newspaper**
- ❖ **Acrylic paints**
- ❖ **Paintbrushes**
- ❖ **Permanent markers (optional)**
- ❖ **Clear acrylic sealer (optional)**

WHAT YOU DO

1 Wipe or wash away any dirt from the rocks. Consider how the different shapes might fit together in a fun or interesting arrangement, such as the burger and pickles shown here. A rock that is dome-shaped on top and flat on the bottom, for example, can make a perfect "bun."

2 Cover your work surface with newspaper. If your rocks are really dark, paint a base coat of white so the colors in your design will look as bright as possible. In most cases, though, painting your design right on the rock will be fine.

3 Let the paint dry completely. To protect your artwork, brush on a coat or two of clear acrylic sealer.

Stone Painting Tricks

* Let the texture of the rock work in your favor. For example, a disk-shaped rock with a rough surface can easily resemble a burger of ground beef once it's painted dark brown.

* Apply blobs of paint to simulate items such as mustard or ketchup. Remember, blobs take longer to dry.

* To give specific shapes (such as pickle seeds) a 3-dimensional look, outline them with a thin line of darker paint or black marker.

Here's The Story

Have you ever walked along a beach or trail and come across a stack of stones balanced just so, one on top of the other? Arranging rocks is an art that goes back to ancient times and continues to inspire artists today. Here are examples of how people from different cultures have stacked stones in the past:

• Centuries ago, the Inuits, who lived in the Arctic region and Alaska, built stone structures for purposes such as marking a dangerous route or a good hunting spot. They even built stone structures to identify a place or thing that could bring good luck.

• Nestled in the woods of southern New Hampshire lies an expansive arrangement of rock caves, tunnels, pillars, and slabs that pose an unsolved puzzle. Some of the standing stones are set in ways that line up with the sunrises and sunsets on the longest day of the year (the solstice) and the on shortest day of the year (the equinox). Carbon dating suggests that parts of the site may be 4,000 years old. Perhaps some unknown Native Americans cut and placed the massive stones, at least one of which is thought to weigh several tons.

Paper PoTLuck

Imagine, if you can, living in a world without paper. No books, magazines, photos, tissues, grocery bags—the list goes on and on. Americans use nearly 200 billion pounds of paper every year!

Over time, paper has been made from a variety of materials. The Egyptians who first invented paper used papyrus reeds that grew along the Nile River. The Greeks used calfskin to make a thin, light type of paper called parchment. Most of the paper we use now is made from wood fibers. This method of papermaking first came from the Chinese.

In the days when paper was less available, it was used mainly for record keeping. But by the late 1700s, papermaking had become big business in Europe and America. Before long, artists were snipping, folding, shaping, curling, and gluing it into all kinds of art forms. On the following pages, you'll discover a potpourri of paper projects inspired by America's early craftsmen.

Paper Cutting

Immigrants from many different countries brought paper-cutting traditions to America. For instance, the French used black paper to cut out portraits which they called *silhouettes*. The Chinese snipped paper and folded it into hanging lanterns to celebrate their New Year. The Mexicans who came to America brought lacy paper flags, a craft learned from the Spanish settlers. And Swiss immigrants brought their tradition of cutting out intricate paper coat of arms they placed on birth certificates and marriage licenses. With so many techniques to choose from, Americans developed further paper art forms, such as paper-doll chains. Cut from paper folded accordion-style, these little figures were also called dancing dollies.

People Chains

Cutting people chains out of folded paper has been a popular pastime for kids in America since Colonial times.

WHAT YOU DO

1 Fold the construction paper accordion-style into thirds or quarters.

2 Draw the outline below on the top fold, making sure the hands and feet extend all the way to the folds. Don't draw the hair.

WHAT YOU NEED

- **Large sheet of construction paper**
- **Pencil**
- **Scissors**
- **Scraps of gift wrap, tissue paper, or scrapbook paper**
- **Tape**
- **Glue stick**
- **Small handful of shredded packing paper (the kind used in shipping boxes)**
- **Stapler**
- **Googly eyes (optional)**

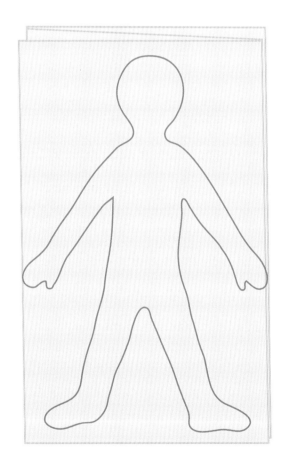

3 Cut along the lines, through all layers, but
don't trim all the way around the fingers
and toes. Remember, the dolls must remain
connected to one another.

4 Unfold the cutout. Cut out pants, shirts, or
dresses from scraps of decorative paper.
Dress the dolls by taping or gluing the
clothes on the dolls.

5 Staple small bunches of shredded packing
paper to the top of the heads or cut out
paper wigs and glue them on. Glue on
googly eyes if you wish.

CRAFT
HINT

Duds and Do's

Put a brand-new spin on this old-
fashioned craft by recycling paper
packing material into curly hairdos and
transforming scraps of printed gift
wrap into cool clothes.

Animal Parade

Instead of creating a people chain, cut out a line-up of linked critters, like these salamanders, and paint or draw on colorful creature features.

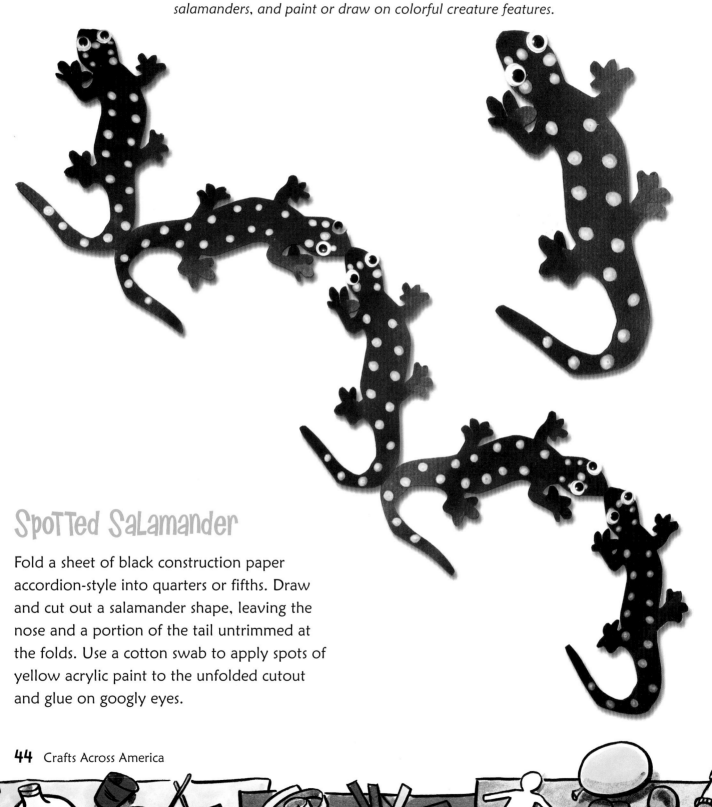

SpoTTed SaLamander

Fold a sheet of black construction paper accordion-style into quarters or fifths. Draw and cut out a salamander shape, leaving the nose and a portion of the tail untrimmed at the folds. Use a cotton swab to apply spots of yellow acrylic paint to the unfolded cutout and glue on googly eyes.

Ducks in a Row

A row of ducks is another creative option for your animal parade.

Fold a piece of white cardstock accordion-style into quarters or fifths. Draw and then cut out a duck shape leaving the beak and tip of the tail feather untrimmed at the folds. Use orange and black markers to color the beaks and feet and to draw on eyes. Finally, fold the feet on each bird toward opposite sides of the body and your ducks are ready to stand upright.

Quack!
Quack!

Hawaiian Leis

Ask anyone to name a symbol of Hawaiian hospitality and they're bound to mention a *lei*. Traditionally, lots of natural items besides flowers have been strung into leis, including leaves, shells, seeds, nuts, and feathers. In the past, Hawaiians would travel into the mountains during molting season to collect feathers shed by island birds.

Over the years, Hawaiian leis have been given as a symbol of peace between leaders, to welcome tourists, to show affection, and to honor accomplishments. During the early 1900s, when most island visitors traveled by boat, it was customary for departing passengers to throw their leis into the sea. The hope was that, like the lei which would wash back ashore, the visitor would return to Hawaii.

Because a lei is a symbol of friendship, it is considered rude to refuse one. It is also disrespectful to remove a lei in front of the person who gave it to you. If someone gives you a lei, be sure to drape it over your shoulders so that part of it hangs in front of you and the other part hangs down your back. That's the Hawaiian way.

ALoha!

Here's The Story

Native Hawaiians are generally believed to be descendants of people from Polynesia. Most historians believe that around AD 400, explorers from the extreme eastern islands of Polynesia—the Marquesas— came in outrigger canoes and settled in the islands of Hawaii. Around 800 years after the first group of settlers arrived, other Polynesians came in their canoes, this time from Tahiti. Their customs and language were also integrated into native Hawaiian life. The custom of making and wearing flower garlands was introduced many centuries ago by these settlers from Tahiti.

Flower Fashion

Hawaiian leis made from fresh flowers, such as orchids, roses, plumeria, or hibiscus, are real treasures, but they only last a few days. To make a garland that will never wilt, cut and fold colorful tissue paper into frilly blossoms that are just as pretty as the real things.

WHAT YOU DO

1 Lay down 3 sheets of tissue paper, stacked on top of each other. Place the jar lid on top and trace around it as many times as it will fit on the paper. Cut out the 3-layer circles with the craft scissors. The number of 3-layer circles you need will depend on the length of your lei.

2 Fold the 3-layer circles in half a series of times to create pleats. Then unfold them.

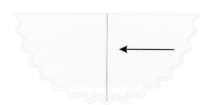

WHAT YOU NEED

- ❖ **Colored or printed tissue paper**
- ❖ **Jar lid or other circular object, about 3 inches in diameter**
- ❖ **Pencil**
- ❖ **Craft scissors or pinking shears with a scalloped edge**
- ❖ **Regular scissors**
- ❖ **2 or 3 drinking straws**
- ❖ **Measuring tape**
- ❖ **Embroidery needle and embroidery floss**
- ❖ **Tape**
- ❖ **Pony beads**

3 Cut the straws into short lengths, about ½ to ¾ inch, to use as spacers.

4 Cut a piece of embroidery floss a few inches longer than the finished size of your lei. Separate 3 strands from the floss. Thread the needle with these 3 strands. Stick a small piece of tape to the other end of the thread to keep the items you're about to sew from falling off.

5 String a bead onto the thread, then a straw spacer, then another bead. Add a paper flower by pushing the needle straight through the center of the 3-layer circle.

6 Continue in this order: bead, spacer, bead, flower. When you have filled the thread, tie the ends of the lei together.

Frilly Edges

Craft scissors will cut paper with many different edge designs. Pinking shears will cut edges with a zigzag edge. But never, never use your mom's good pinking shears on paper. The paper will dull the shears.

So What's Polynesia?

Polynesia is a word for a scattered group of islands in the eastern and southeastern Pacific Ocean. These islands lie from New Zealand, north to Hawaii, and east to Easter Island.

Polish Paper Craft

Using a simplified version of a Polish paper-cutting technique called wycinanki, *you can make a branch of fancy paper leaves. Hang your finished mobile in front of a window where you can watch the foliage flutter in the breeze.*

WHAT YOU NEED

❖ **Lightweight laminating sheets (optional)**
❖ **Green scrapbook paper**
❖ **Ruler**
❖ **Marker**
❖ **Regular scissors**
❖ **Craft scissors**
❖ **Flexible copper craft wire**
❖ **Fishing swivel**
❖ **Clear packing tape**

WHAT YOU DO

1 If you are using laminating sheets, laminate several pieces of green paper. Use the edge of the ruler to press out any air bubbles. If you find this step difficult, ask a grownup to help you.

2 Cut the green paper into 5 x 3-inch rectangles. Fold each rectangle in half lengthwise and run the edge of the ruler along the fold to make a sharp crease.

3 Use the marker to draw half of a simple rounded leaf shape with a stem (make this thicker than usual) on each folded rectangle, using the crease for the center.

4 Cut out the shape, cutting on the inner edge of the marker line. Do not cut the fold. Use regular scissors for the stem portion and craft scissors for the rest. Cut several thin grooves down from the crease into the leaf to resemble veins.

5 To shape a branch for your leaves, cut a 30-inch length of craft wire. Thread the loop end of a fishing swivel onto the wire, slide it to the center, then twist the wire ends together a few times just below the swivel. Spread the wire ends apart. Attach a leaf to the end of each branch by folding the stem around the wire and wrapping a piece of packing tape around it.

6 Cut a 4-inch length of wire for each of the remaining leaves. Tape each stem to one end of a wire. Twist the other end around the branch. Repeat for each stem. Space the leaves evenly apart.

Wycinanki Folk Art

In Poland, farming families traditionally decorated the walls of their homes with hand-painted or stenciled designs. When new dyes were developed in the 1800s along with shiny colored paper, Polish families traded their paintbrushes for scissors.

They cut out elaborate images to post on ceiling beams and along the tops of walls. These designs, called *wycinanki*, were symmetrical, meaning the sides were mirror images of each other. *Wycinanki* didn't last as long as painted stencils; so each year, during spring cleaning, the farm wives took down the old cutouts and set about snipping new ones. When these families immigrated to America in the late 1800s, they brought the art of *wycinanki* with them to decorate their new homes.

The Art of Quilling

This unique craft may be called quilling, but there are no porcupines involved—just narrow coils of paper pinched into a variety of shapes and arranged into all sorts of interesting designs. The name *quill* comes from earlier days when the paper strips were likely rolled around the quill of a feather.

Quilling has been around for more than 500 years, and it is actually a spin-off of *filigree*—the art of bending silver and gold wire into fragile, open designs. In the late 1700s, when paper became more available and, of course, far less expensive than silver and gold, quilling really became a popular hobby. In England, women used quilling to spruce up baskets, trays, and furniture. From England, quilling spread to colonial New England where the art was even taught in some schools.

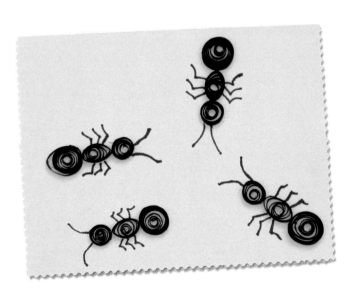

CurLicue-CriTTer GreeTing

At first glance, quilling may look a little puzzling; but it's really a cinch to get into the swing (make that spin) of it. Nowadays there's a slotted needle-like tool designed just for rolling up thin paper strips, although you can achieve similar results using a toothpick or a kitchen skewer. If you want to make large, looser coils, you can even use a pencil. Try your hand at making the shapes on the next page. Then you can piece them together to create a unique greeting card.

WHAT YOU NEED

- ❖ **Colored cardstock or scrapbook paper**
- ❖ **Craft scissors (optional)**
- ❖ **Pencil**
- ❖ **Scrap paper**
- ❖ **Regular scissors**
- ❖ **Craft glue**
- ❖ **Ruler**
- ❖ **Various colored paper to cut as quilling strips**
- ❖ **Toothpicks or quilling tool**
- ❖ **Craft glue**
- ❖ **Colored markers**

WHAT YOU DO

1 Fold a piece of colored paper in half to make the card. If you want a decorative edge, trim the edges with craft scissors.

2 Sketch out a design or scene on a piece of paper the same size as your greeting card.

3 If your design includes a background, such as a grassy hill, cut the pieces out of colored paper and glue them onto the card.

4 If you are not using commercial quilling strips, cut paper strips ⅛ inch wide and 12 inches long. Practice quilling with a few of these strips. Tightly wrap a strip around a toothpick. If you are using a commercial quilling tool, slip the end of a strip into the groove in the tip of the quilling tool and roll the paper into a coil. Gently remove the coil. Let your coil loosen a bit, then use a drop of glue to hold the loose end in place.

5 Use your practice coils to try making other shapes. (See examples below.) Make the pieces you need for your design and glue them in place. Add finer details to your design with the markers. Write your personal greeting inside the card.

Equipped for Quilling

Quilling strips (long 1/8-inch wide strips of craft paper) and tools are sold in most art and craft supply stores. Or you can cut your own paper strips and use a toothpick or similar item around which to roll them.

V Scroll

Fold a quilling strip in half then roll each end to the outside. Glue folded section together.

Circle

Don't pinch the coil, and you have a circle.

Shaped Teardrop

Pinch the top and curl it to make a shaped teardrop.

Pointed Oval

Pinch the top and bottom to create a pointed oval.

Teardrop

Pinch the top and you have a teardrop.

Triangle

Pinch three points to form a triangle.

Shape It Up

*Make up your own designs, or try your
hand at some of these.*

ANTS-eee!

For each ant, roll a 12-inch strip into a circle for
the back segment. Use 6-inch strips to shape a
pointed oval shape for the midsection and a
circle for the head. Draw legs and antennae on
the paper with a black marker.

Field Flower

For each blossom, use an 8-inch strip to shape
each petal into a pointed oval shape. Use a
4-inch strip to make a circle center. Add
uncoiled strips for flower stems.

Curly Top Carrot

Use four 6-inch orange strips to make 4 shaped teardrops. Use one 6-inch orange strip to make a triangle for the carrot end on the bottom. For the carrot top, use two 6-inch green strips to make two closed V scrolls.

Bouncy Bunny

For a bunny, shape two 12-inch white strips into pointed ovals for ears. The body is made from a 24-inch strip shaped into a circle. Use an 8-inch strip to form a teardrop for the head and a 4-inch strip to form a circle for the tail. Shape an 8-inch strip into a pointed oval for the foot.

English Immigrants

When the English came to America, they settled along the Eastern seacoast; and between 1607 and 1733, they formed thirteen colonies: Virginia, Massachusetts, New Hampshire, Connecticut, New Jersey, New York, Rhode Island, Maryland, Delaware, Pennsylvania, North Carolina, South Carolina, and Georgia.

Kids who lived in the early British colonies had lots to do. Boys helped their fathers hunt and plant crops while girls had household jobs, such as making candles and soap, spinning and weaving wool, and helping prepare meals.

Besides their daily chores, some children also went to school. Usually, the first schools they attended were in the teachers' homes. The students studied their letters and numbers while their female teachers did their housework. These elementary schools were known as Dame Schools because women were typically called dames back then. After finishing Dame School, boys often graduated to grammar school but girls stayed home to help their mothers.

Having Fun Colonial Style

With all of their responsibilities, kids still squeezed in time for a little fun now and then. They played games, such as checkers, leapfrog, or hopscotch. On a windy day, they might fly kites. During winter snowfalls, they most likely slid down snowy hills on sleds they made out of wood scraps.

Quilling Tips

* Gently tear a quilling strip to the length you need rather than cutting it. This will create a softer looking edge once the strip is glued in place.
* To make gluing easier, pour a little glue into a jar lid and use a toothpick to apply it to the coils.
* Keep a damp paper towel handy for wiping your fingertips when they get sticky.

Mosaic Masterpieces

You don't need stone or tile to piece together a colorful mosaic. Cut magazine pictures or scrapbook paper into squares, then glue them into a design on a plain notebook cover. You'll have a one-of-a-kind journal or sketchbook!

WHAT YOU DO

1 Cut a piece of scrap paper about the size of the notebook or journal cover and sketch a design for your mosaic. When you are satisfied with your design, lightly redraw it on the book cover. Or if you wish, you can cut out the pieces of the design and trace around them on your cover.

2 Sort the glossy paper by color. Don't be shy about using different patterns in similar hues. It will look great when you're done.

3 Cut the paper into thin strips. Then cut the strips into small square or triangular "tiles."

4 Apply glue to a small portion of the design and arrange paper tiles on top, spacing them slightly apart. If you need to move a tile once you've positioned it, use a toothpick to slowly push or slide it into place. Gently press down on the pieces with your fingertips to stick them in place. Continue gluing on tiles, a section at a time. If necessary, trim the edges to fit. Before you know it, your whole design will be filled in.

WHAT YOU NEED

- ❖ **Scissors**
- ❖ **Scrap paper**
- ❖ **Notebook or journal with a plain cover**
- ❖ **Pencil and paper**
- ❖ **Glossy paper, such as gift wrap or magazine pictures**
- ❖ **Glue stick**
- ❖ **Toothpicks**

Here's The Story

More than 2,000 years ago, Mediterranean homebuilders grew tired of having dirt floors, so they spread cement mortar over the dirt and pressed stone chips into it. Not only was this new flooring neat and clean, it also felt cool underfoot. The Romans continued to develop this simple tiling technique, eventually decorating their villas, temples, and baths with elaborate mosaic patterns created out of marble and colored glass—even silver and gold. As their empire grew, the Romans brought the art of mosaics to other parts of the world. Centuries later, it would be the Italians who created many of America's first stone carvings and mosaics.

In the late 1800s, Italians began immigrating to America in great numbers. Many of those who had been farmers in their homeland had to find new kinds of jobs—working in factories and mines or as laborers building railroads and subways. Those who came from southern Italy, where stone was a more common building material than wood, were often hired as stonecutters, tile setters, and masons. As American cities such as Philadelphia, New York, Cleveland, and Indianapolis continued to grow, their skills were in high demand. Much of these immigrants' early handiwork remains a highlight of those cities today.

So What's a Roman?

A *Roman* is a citizen of Rome today or a citizen of the ancient Roman Empire.

CRAFT HINT

Come Un-glued

When working with mosaics, keep a damp paper towel handy for wiping off any glue that gets on your fingers while you work.

Japanese Origami

Traditional Japanese kimonos are made of silk and worn for special occasions. During a wedding, for instance, the bride will dress in a beautifully embroidered white kimono while her groom wears a black silk one decorated with the family crest. Properly wrapping and tying a kimono can take an hour or so. With this origami pattern, it only takes a few quick folds to outfit a whole collection of wooden spoon dolls in fancy paper robes.

WHAT YOU NEED

- ❖ **Wooden craft spoon**
- ❖ **2-inch square black paper**
- ❖ **Pencil**
- ❖ **Scissors**
- ❖ **Glue stick**
- ❖ **1 4½-inch square colored or printed paper**
- ❖ **1 4½ by ⅛-inch strip from colored or printed paper**
- ❖ **Permanent fine-tip marker**

WHAT YOU DO

1 Place the wide end of the craft spoon on top of the black paper square. Draw a hairdo around the spoon and cut it out. If you want a style with bangs, simply fold down the top ½ inch of the paper before you start. Glue the cutout to the spoon.

2 For the kimono, place the 4½-inch paper square right side up on a flat surface. Fold down the top ¼ inch, then flip the paper over.

3 Apply glue to the back of the spoon handle. Center it on top of the paper (the doll's head should be above the fold). Press down to stick in place. Following the diagrams, fold down the right shoulder and then the left.

4 Next, make a second pair of overlapping folds below the first pair. Glue the overlap in place, if needed.

5 For a sash (traditionally called an *obi*), wrap the paper strip around the kimono from front to back and glue the overlapping edges together.

6 Use the marker to draw the face.

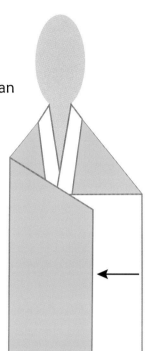

So What's an Obi?

An *obi* is the very long, broad sash tied around the waist of a kimono. The knot used to tie the obi depends upon the occasion.

Here's The Story

With drawing and painting, it's what you put on the paper that makes art. With *origami*, the paper itself becomes art. You just have to fold it the right way to make the art emerge.

Paper folding has been a favorite form of art in Japan for more than a thousand years, yet no written instructions were printed until 1797, when a man named Akisato Rito published a book of models called *Sembazuru Orikata*. The title, which means *How to Fold One-Thousand Cranes*, is based on the Japanese belief that if, when you have a wish, you fold a thousand flapping birds, the wish will be granted.

Folding, or *sembazuru*, was a tradition practiced by Japanese brides who hoped for a long and successful marriage. In the 1960s Japanese Americans living in Hawaii adopted sembazuru as a way of celebrating their heritage, and the custom became popular once more. But instead of folding 1,000 cranes, the custom was changed to fold 1,001. Odd numbers are considered lucky by the Japanese.

Papier-Mâché

At first glance, paper might seem like flimsy stuff; but soak it in a bit of watery glue, mold it into a shape, and when it dries, it will be really hard and strong. That is papier-mâché. For centuries papier-mâché was used in Europe and Asia to shape everything from doll heads and chessboards to lampshades and furniture. English immigrants brought the art to America. George Washington even had the ceilings of his Mount Vernon home decorated with papier-mâché.

It was only a matter of time before American craftsmen mastered their own form of the art. In the mid 1800s, an Englishman named William Allgood started the Litchfield Manufacturing Company of Connecticut, which became famous all around the world for its papier-mâché clock cases.

Papier-mâché Paste

This recipe makes an especially smooth paste that's nice to work with, but it requires using boiling water. Be sure to ask your parents for permission or help before making it.

WHAT YOU NEED

- ❖ **4 cups water, divided**
- ❖ **½ cup flour**
- ❖ **3 tablespoons sugar**

WHAT YOU DO

1 In a medium bowl, combine 2 cups of water and flour. Stir to mix well. Set aside. In a small saucepan, pour the remaining 2 cups of water and bring to a boil. Ask a grownup for help or permission before boiling the water.

2 Lower the heat and carefully stir the flour mixture into the hot water. Turn the heat back on until the mixture just starts to bubble.

3 Remove pan from heat and stir in the sugar. Pour the mixture into a plastic bowl to cool and thicken. Once cool, the paste is ready to use.

Papier Pals

Animals are especially fun to shape out of papier-mâché. Start by building a rough body shape out of cardboard and plastic recyclables, then flesh out the figure with the mâché.

WHAT YOU NEED

- **Papier-mâché Paste (recipe on page 63)**
- **Recyclable containers, egg cartons, oatmeal canisters, paper cups**
- **Bamboo skewers or chopsticks**
- **Scissors**
- **Lots of newspaper or newsprint**
- **Masking tape**
- **Wooden beads or balls for eyes**
- **Acrylic paints**
- **Paintbrushes**

WHAT YOU DO

1 Prepare a batch of Papier-mâché Paste.

2 While the paste cools, create a base for your animal by taping together different containers and supplies and using scrunched newspaper for filler.

If you're making a pig, use a 2-liter plastic bottle for a body. For each leg, cut 2 cups from an egg carton and fit one inside the other. The ears and tail can be fashioned

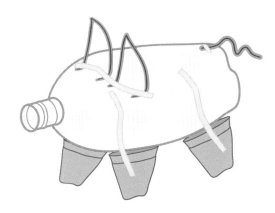

out of twist ties and tape.

For a horse, poke 4 kitchen skewers or bamboo chopsticks into the side of an oatmeal canister for legs. Wrap them with newspaper and tape. Add egg carton cups, flipped upside down, for hooves. Poke a skewer into the front of the canister for the neck. Tape on scrunched newspaper to fill out the neck. Fashion a head out of paper cups and more scrunched newspaper. Top it off with ears as described for the pig.

3 Tear more newspaper into long, thin strips. One at a time, dip them into the paste, then gently run them between your fingers to squeeze off extra paste and stick them onto the animal's frame. Cover the whole body with at least 3 layers of strips. Put the eyes (painted wooden beads work well) in place when you're halfway through so you can hold them in place with pasted strips for eyelids. Add other elements such as raffia, jute, or yarn for a horse's forelock, mane, and tail with the last layer (see photo).

4 Let your animal dry overnight so the paste is completely dry and firm. Paint your animal. It may take a few coats to cover the newspaper print.

Chili Pepper Piñata

Using papier-mâché, mold a piñata in any number of interesting forms, like a giant chili pepper with nooks and crannies to fill with candies. It will be the hit of the party for sure! You can also hang it as a party decoration. Or hang the piñata from your bedroom ceiling for a room decoration. In this case, leave it empty so you won't be tempted to break it.

WHAT YOU NEED

❖ **Papier-mâché Paste (recipe on page 63)**
❖ **2 large round party balloons**
❖ **Masking tape**
❖ **Plenty of newspapers**
❖ **Straight pin**
❖ **Wrapped hard candies and small toys or trinkets, optional**
❖ **String or cord**
❖ **Acrylic paints and paintbrushes**

WHAT YOU DO

1 Prepare a batch of Papier-mâché Paste.

2 While the paste cools, blow up 1 balloon as full as possible. Blow up the other balloon only about 3/4 full. Tape the 2 balloons together.

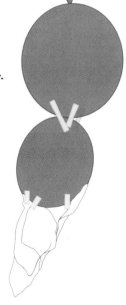

3 Scrunch up some newspaper to form a tapered tip and tape it to the bottom of the smaller balloon.

4 Tear more newspapers into long, thin strips. One at a time, dip the strips into the paste, gently run them between your fingers to squeeze off extra paste, and wrap them around the chili pepper frame. Apply at least 3 layers of papier-mâché strips, leaving a small opening near the top for putting in the candy.

5 Let the chili pepper dry overnight.

6 Use a pin to pop the balloons. If you wish, fill the *piñata* with candy.

7 Knot 1 end of a long piece of string or cord and tape the knot to the top of the *piñata* beside the opening. Cover the hole and the knot with papier-mâché and it dry.

8 Paint the chili pepper bright red with a green stem top. Let it dry overnight, then hang your piñata.

Here's The Story

The Spanish brought the piñata to the New World in the 1500s. They learned about piñatas from the Italians, who themselves got the idea from the Chinese. Even then it would be a while before it became the birthday party hit it is today.

Missionaries first introduced it to the Mexicans as a centerpiece for Christian holidays, such as the *Posada* celebration of Mary and Joseph's journey to Bethlehem. Traditionally, piñatas were in the shape of a donkey, which was in honor of the burro Mary rode to Bethlehem. Stars, fish, and birds were also common shapes. The piñata's contents—candies, fruits, and jewelry—symbolized temptations that could be destroyed by breaking the container into pieces with a stick.

CoLorfuL CoLLage

Looking for a way to brighten up your room? All you need is some colored paper and glue to transform a plain lampshade into an amazing collage. When you turn on the switch, the spotlight will be on your work of art.

WHAT YOU NEED

- ❖ **Newspaper**
- ❖ **Wax paper**
- ❖ **Green mulberry paper or crafting tissue paper (the kind that doesn't bleed when it gets wet)**
- ❖ **Scissors**
- ❖ **Small lamp with a plain shade**
- ❖ **Mod Podge sealer/glue**
- ❖ **Small paintbrush**
- ❖ **2 toothpicks**
- ❖ **Seed beads**

WHAT YOU DO

1 Cover your work surface with newspaper topped with wax paper.

2 Cut green paper into strips about 4 inches high and 8 to 12 inches long. Cut enough strips to go all the way around the lower edge of the lampshade with a little overlap between pieces. Cut wide grass blades into the upper portion of each strip and leave 1 inch along the bottom uncut to hold it all together.

3 One at a time, place the grass strips right side down on the wax paper and paint the uncut edge with Mod Podge. Carefully lift the strip and press the glued portion in place along the bottom of the lampshade. At this point, the grass blades will droop down. Glue

about half of them to the shade. Attach the others after the fish are on. Trim the last strip to slightly overlap the first.

4 Cut out paper fish, as many shapes and colors as you want. Glue them to the shade, facing both directions. Position the fish on top of and between the glued-on grass blades.

5 To add an eye to each fish, apply a dot of glue with a toothpick. Slip a seed bead onto the tip of another toothpick and gently press it into the glue.

6 Glue down the loose grass blades. Cover parts of the fish to give your design a three-dimensional look. Allow the glue to dry. Turn on the lamp to light up your underwater scene.

Pushing The Envelope

There's an expression called "pushing the envelope" that is used to describe something or someone who takes things beyond the usual. That's what artists Pablo Picasso and Georges Braque did. While they were living in France in the early 1900s, they developed a new style of art by taking objects apart and then fitting the pieces back together in brand new and unexpected ways. This was the beginning of collage.

Not long afterward, Robert Rauschenberg, an American of German and Cherokee descent, went to study art in Paris. When he came home, he started working on giant three-dimensional collages made of a variety of junkyard objects. One of his most famous creations included the heel of a shoe, a tennis ball, a tire, and a stuffed goat!

So What's Collage?

Collage is a word that comes from the French word for pasting or gluing and means a picture made by gluing several objects into a new arrangement.

Woven Reed Baskets

Instead of using splints of wood to make a Native American–style basket, you can easily cut and fold gift wrap or colored paper into long, thin strips—enough to weave a whole collection of decorative containers for stashing trinkets, baseball cards, or other treasures.

WHAT YOU NEED

* **Ruler**
* **Empty box, the size of the basket you want to make**
* **Pencil and paper**
* **Scissors**
* **Heavyweight colored paper or gift wrap**
* **Glue stick**
* **Decorative paper punch (optional)**

WHAT YOU DO

1 Measure the height of 2 sides and the bottom of the box. Write down the measurements and add the 3 numbers together. Cut strips from the colored paper, each as long as your measurement and ½ to 1 inch wide. If you're using gift wrap that is printed on one side only, cut the strips 3 times as wide. Fold them into thirds and glue down the open edge. These are your reeds.

2 Lay down enough reeds to cover the box bottom. Lay these side by side on a flat surface. Weave more reeds over and under these in an alternating pattern, as shown. Slide these reeds close enough so they touch each other.

3 Glue the overlapping reeds in each of the 4 corners. Set the box on top of the paper to help you shape the basket. Crease the reeds at the base of the box so the sides stand up. These will be the spokes of your basket.

4 Measure all the way around your box and write this measurement down. Cut out more reeds this length or glue two reeds together. Glue the end of 1 of these reeds to the base of 1 spoke. Weave the reed in and out of the other spokes all the way around the basket. Trim the reed at a point that slightly overlaps the starting point and glue the reed in place.

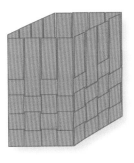

5 Weave in more reeds, making sure that each new row is on the opposite sides of the spokes. Once your basket starts to hold its shape, remove the box.

6 After you have woven the final row, fold down the top of the spokes. Fold the spokes that are in front of the upper reed over the reed and into the basket. Fold the spokes that are behind the top strip over the reed and to the outside. Trim the ends and glue them in place.

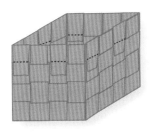

7 Decorate your basket. You can use a paper punch to create decorative shapes and glue them onto your basket.

Here's The Story

Before the colonists arrived, Native Americans wove baskets out of a variety of natural materials, such as birch bark, cattails, cornhusks, and sweet grass. By the 1600s, they were using ash splints for their baskets. The Native Americans probably learned about this way of weaving baskets from Swedish settlers.

Eventually the Nipmucs, one of the Native American tribes of central New England, began selling splint baskets to support their families. They would weave the splints over carved wooden blocks to make sure the baskets were nicely shaped. Then they used paints made from berries to decorate the baskets with dots, leaves, and other symbols.

Mardi Gras Masks

The traditional Mardi Gras colors—purple for justice, green for faith, and gold for power—were selected more than one hundred years ago by the King of the Carnival. Using assorted paper in those colors, you can design a popular feather-style mask to celebrate the holiday in style.

Here's The Story

Each year, between February and March, New Orleans hosts the Mardi Gras carnival, with dozens of parades and elaborate costume balls. The festivities end promptly at midnight on Fat Tuesday, which is the day before the first day of Lent. Mardi Gras is celebrated in a number of countries; but in America, it was first observed in 1699 by French explorers on the banks of the Mississippi River.

One of the biggest highlights of the festival is catching the aluminum coins, called *doubloons*, and shiny necklaces that are tossed from the floats and balconies. To attract the attention of those who throw the coins and beads, many people spend the day in disguise, wearing full costumes or masks made of feathers, sequins, or glitter.

WHAT YOU NEED

- ❖ **Wooden paint stirrer**
- ❖ **Purple craft paint**
- ❖ **Paintbrush**
- ❖ **Pencil**
- ❖ **Thin cardboard or file folder**
- ❖ **Paper scissors**
- ❖ **Craft scissors**
- ❖ **Purple, green, and gold or yellow colored papers**
- ❖ **Glue stick**

WHAT YOU DO

1 Paint the stirrer with purple paint; set aside to dry.

2 Sketch a mask shape on the cardboard or folder and cut it out.

3 Use the craft scissors to cut out colored paper feathers, some long enough to extend beyond the edge of the cardboard and others small enough to fit on top of the mask.

4 Glue the feathers to the mask. Start with the larger feathers and work all the way around both eyeholes. Do not cover the center section between the eyeholes.

5 Glue smaller feathers on top of the larger ones, this time covering the space between the eyeholes.

6 Glue the stirrer to the back of the cardboard for a handle.

So What's Lent?

Lent is the forty days before Easter when many people give up something in preparation for the message of Easter.

Alaskan Sunglasses

At first glance, the narrow eye slits of Inuit snow goggles might look odd, but they are designed to limit the amount of sunlight and reflective glare that reaches your eyes. That is important in a land that is covered with snow. To see how well the glasses work, try making a pair of your own out of cardboard.

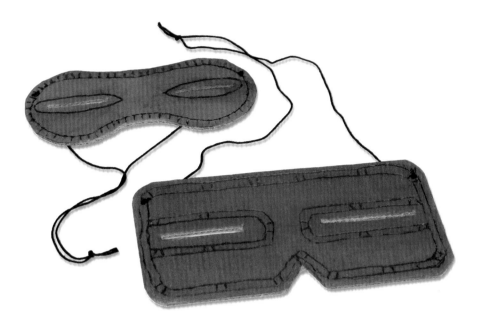

WHAT YOU NEED

- ❖ **Pencil**
- ❖ **Cardboard rectangle, 3½ x 7 inches**
- ❖ **Craft knife**
- ❖ **Light-colored crayon**
- ❖ **Finish nail or paper clip**
- ❖ **Black watercolor paint and paintbrush**
- ❖ **Tissues**
- ❖ **Scissors**
- ❖ **Sewing elastic**

WHAT YOU DO

1 Sketch a pair of goggles on the cardboard. Round the edges and make a notch for your nose. Or trace around a large jar lid to create a pair of circles spaced 1 inch apart. Connect them with a curved line at the top and bottom. Draw narrow eye slits, no more than ¼ inch wide.

2 Cut out the goggles, including the eye slits, with the craft knife. Ask a grownup for help or permission to do this.

3 Color the face of the goggles with crayon. The thicker you apply the color, the better your design will look.

4 With the tip of a nail or straightened paper clip, draw a border on the goggles. The aim is to scratch off the crayon, so be sure to apply enough pressure. Gently brush or blow off any crayon shavings.

5 Brush a coat of black watercolor paint over the goggles. Wait a few minutes, then gently blot the surface of the goggles with a damp tissue to remove excess paint.

6 Use the nail or paper clip to poke a hole in the upper corner of each side of the goggles. Thread 1 piece of sewing elastic through each hole. Knot both ends so the elastic won't pull through the goggles. Tie the ends together, adjusting the length to fit.

Protect Your Eyes!

Decorate the edges of your sunglasses with a traditional design. Remember, though, no matter what style of sunglasses you wear, never look directly at the sun.

Here's The Story

Alaska became our forty-ninth state in 1958, but for centuries before, the Inuits had lived as nomads, following the seal, caribou, polar bear, and whale. They depended on these animals for food and skins. Everyday and ceremonial items—such as snow goggles, wrist guards, and burial masks—were often carved out of walrus tusks and then decorated with an engraved border. To accent their carvings, the Inuits filled in the grooves with soot. The types of shelter the Inuits built depended on the season. In the summer, they would pitch tents, which they made from animal skins draped over wooden poles or whalebones. Their winter homes were built of sod or snow and ice.

While the Inuit men hunted meat, the women and children gathered roots, berries, seeds, and nuts. Sometimes they ground wheat and other wild grains into flour. In more recent times, Bannock bread, sometimes called Eskimo donuts, became a popular treat. It's made by wrapping dough around a stick and holding it over a campfire to cook.

Things With Strings

On the side of Highway 24 in Cawker City, Kansas, sits the world's largest ball of twine. In 1953, a farmer named Frank Stoeber began rolling up spare bits of cord. When he passed away twenty-one years later, the townsfolk carried on the tradition in his memory. Today the ball has a circumference of 40 feet and contains more than 7.8 million feet of twine.

When it comes to creative things to do with twine, cord, floss, yarn, and laces, there are plenty of ways to get the ball rolling. On the following pages are instructions for knotting cotton thread into Guatemalan-style bracelets, weaving yarn into Navajo tapestries, lacing rawhide the cowboy way, and a string of other inventive traditions that wound up in America.

Macramé

Worldwide Traveler

Mention the word *macramé*, and a lot of people think of the 1960s, when the hippie generation knotted yards of twine into groovy plant hangers and hip belts. Take a giant step back in time, though, say 600 years or more, and you will discover that macramé was a technique used to decorate plain cloth with knotted borders. In the 1800s British and American sailors whiled away the hours offshore turning knots and hitches into netting, mats, wheel covers, and sea chest handles.

So What's Macramé?

Macramé, which means "fringe" in the Arabic language, is a way of decorating with knotted string.

Dandy Dragonfly

It's really a cinch to create a shimmery dragonfly like this one. All you need is some cord and a couple of beads.

WHAT YOU NEED

* ❖ **Scissors**
* ❖ **Measuring tape**
* ❖ **Cord**
* ❖ **Small beads**

WHAT YOU DO

1 Cut a 48-inch piece of cord and fold it in half. Tie the ends together with an overhand knot about 3 inches from the fold. (See page 7.)

2 For the dragonfly's eyes, slide a bead onto each end and then push them up against the knot.

3 Cross the right strand over the body and under the left strand. Then slide the left strand under the body and through the loop in the right strand. Pull tight.

4 Repeat step 3, starting with the left strand this time to complete a square knot.

5 To form wings, tie the first half of another square knot but don't pull it tight. Instead, leave a set of

loops that measure about 2½ inches across. Then tie the second part of the square knot and slide it up against the first knot. Repeat this step to create a second, slightly smaller, set of wings. Pull on the ends of each set of wings to tighten the knots.

6 Continue tying square knots down the length of the body, stopping a little way from the end. Thread the ends of the cord through the loop at the tip of the body and trim them short.

Wearable Wings

Turn your dragonfly into a fashionable accessory by gluing it onto a pin back or barrette clasp.

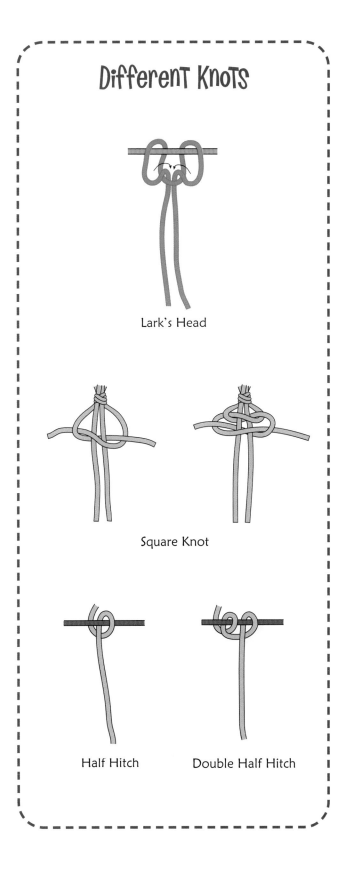

Different Knots

Lark's Head

Square Knot

Half Hitch   Double Half Hitch

Friendship Bracelets

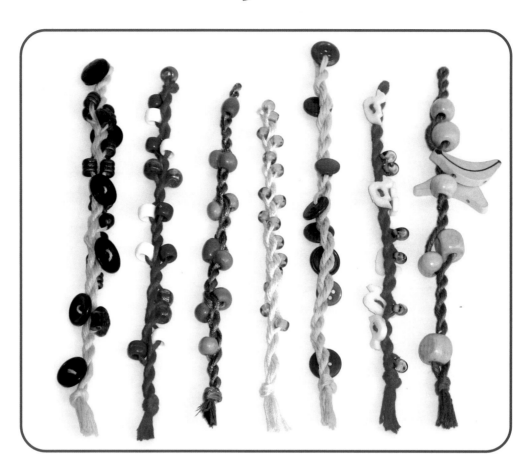

Here's The Story

During the 1970s, kids began swapping colorful, knotted bracelets as tokens of their friendship. The recipient wore the wristband until the strings wore out and broke on their own. Doing so entitled the wearer to make a wish that was supposed to come true once the bracelet fell off.

Many of the striped and checkered designs of the bracelets resemble those found in Native American art. Originally, the bracelets were crafted from dyed and twisted plant fibers. Today, they are typically made using colorful strands of embroidery floss.

Dangle Bangles

These charm-style friendship bracelets are so much fun to make, you'll want to give them to all your pals—and keep one or two to wear yourself. Fashion them out of buttons, beads, or just about anything you can thread onto string.

WHAT YOU NEED

- ❖ **Measuring tape**
- ❖ **Embroidery floss**
- ❖ **Scissors**
- ❖ **Tape**
- ❖ **Beads or buttons**

WHAT YOU DO

1 Measure your wrist to determine the length of bracelet you want. You will probably want your bracelet to be about 2 inches bigger than your wrist. For example, if your wrist measures 6 inches around, you'll probably want your bracelet to be at least 8 inches long. Cut 6 pieces of embroidery floss that are 2½ times the length of the bracelet you want to make. For example, if you want an 8-inch bracelet, you would need to cut 20-inch lengths of floss.

2 Arrange the 6 lengths into a bunch and tape one end securely to the edge of a tabletop.

3 String buttons or beads spaced 1 inch or so apart on one or more of the embroidery floss lengths. If the buttonholes are too small, try unraveling a piece of floss and separating 2 or 3 strands.

4 Gather the free ends of the floss together and twist all 6 strands until you have a thin, tight rope.

5 Continue to hold the end firmly in one hand. Pinch the center of the rope with the other hand, then bring the 2 ends of the rope together. Let go of the middle and the strand will quickly twist around itself to form your bracelet.

6 Tie the ends together with an overhand knot. Wrap your bracelet around your wrist and slip the knot through the loop at the other end.

Worry Dolls

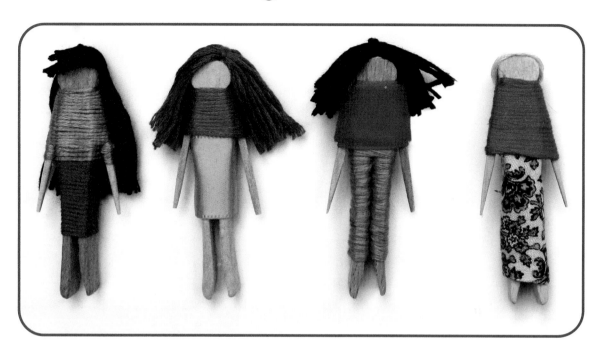

Here's The Story

By the late 1800s, Spanish colonists had settled in southern Texas. Native tribes in these regions shared some of their customs with the Spaniards. One custom was that if you tell your troubles to tiny dolls and tuck them under your pillow, when morning comes, your worries will be gone. This custom began with an ancient Mayan legend:

There was once a family who sold vegetables and handmade cloth. One year a drought came, so the vegetables died. Then a stranger stole their cloth. The daughter collected twigs, made little dolls, and dressed them with scraps of leftover fabric. At night the little girl told her worries to the dolls.

The girl took the dolls to market, but no one bought them. She was about to leave when a man arrived and bought them all. As the little girl raced home with the money, thunder marked the end of the drought, and the thief returned their cloth and apologized. The little worry dolls had performed their magic by taking away all of the family's troubles.

CLOThESPiN PaLS

These worry dolls are bigger than traditional Guatemalan dolls, which makes them easier to fashion. Instead of tucking them under your pillow, stand them on your nightstand.

and glue the halves to the sides of a clothespin. Stretch a rubber band around the pieces to hold in place until the glue dries.

2 To dress your doll, wrap embroidery floss around the clothespin and arms, gluing down the ends of each strand (the tip of a toothpick comes in handy for this). You can also use ribbon, lace, or strips of fabric to create clothes (see photos on previous page).

WHAT YOU NEED

- ❖ **Wooden toothpicks**
- ❖ **Wooden flat-style clothespins (smaller craft-size clothespins work especially well)**
- ❖ **Tacky glue**
- ❖ **Rubber bands**
- ❖ **Embroidery floss**
- ❖ **Ribbon, lace, or fabric scraps**

WHAT YOU DO

1 For each doll, break a toothpick in half

3 For hair, cut a group of short lengths from the embroidery floss and tightly tie them together in the middle with another piece of floss. If you want curly hair, unravel the threads in each strand. Glue the knotted middle to the clothespin top. Arrange the floss around the doll's head, using a little more glue to hold it in place. Trim the front to create bangs.

String-Snap Stamps

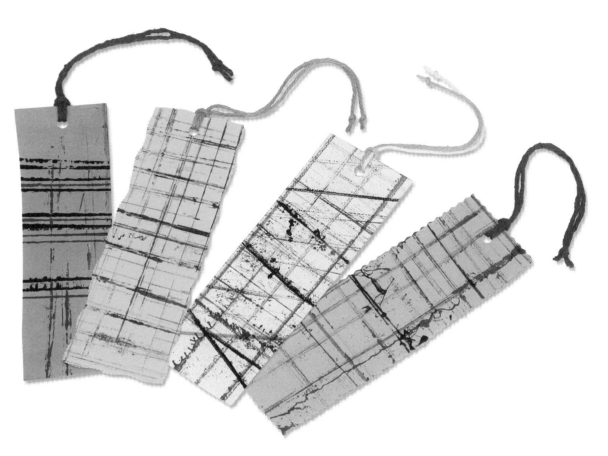

Here's The Story

In Hawaii, islanders made cloth from the bark of paper mulberry trees and used it for clothes. This type of bark cloth, called *kapa*, was decorated with dyes made from coal, clay, and plants. One technique was to dip string into the color and then snap it against the fabric to print a crisscross of straight and diagonal lines.

Kapa became the fashionable cloth for making *muumuus*, a billowy, loose-fitting dress introduced by missionaries in the early 1800s to Hawaiian women. Originally, these plain-looking muumuus featured long sleeves and hems. The Hawaiians shortened the hems and sleeves, dyed the fabrics bright colors, and printed them with striking patterns.

Snappy Bookmarks

The Hawaiian method of decorating kapa cloth can be used to print distinctive patterns on paper too. And you can cut the finished sheets into bookmarks and note cards.

WHAT YOU NEED

- ❖ **Newspapers**
- ❖ **Scissors**
- ❖ **Cardboard**
- ❖ **String**
- ❖ **Construction paper or solid scrapbook paper**
- ❖ **Acrylic paints**
- ❖ **Container to put paint in**
- ❖ **Paintbrush**
- ❖ **Damp paper towel for wiping your fingers**

WHAT YOU DO

1 Cover your work surface with newspapers. Cut a series of ½-inch deep notches in the edges of the cardboard.

2 Cut a piece of string a few inches longer than the cardboard. Knot one end and slide the string into one of the notches so that the knot rests against the back of the board. Place a sheet of construction paper on top of the cardboard.

3 Holding the unknotted end, raise the string and paint it. Then slide the loose end into a notch on the opposite side of the cardboard but continue to hold onto it to keep it taut. Now lift the string and let it snap back down to print a line across the paper.

4 Move the knotted end to another notch, repaint the string, and snap another line. Continue this way to print a crisscross pattern of lines, using a new piece of string for each color (see diagram below).

The Come-Back Toy

In 1928, Pedro Flores, a Filipino immigrant living in California, opened the Yo-Yo Manufacturing Company and put a brand new spin on an age-old toy. Instead of tying the string to the yo-yo's axle, he looped it around. Tied to the axle, the yo-yo could only go up and down, but Flores's yo-yos could rotate or "sleep" at the end of the string. Yo-yoing turned into such a popular craze that, only a year later, the business Flores had started with a dozen hand-carved yo-yos was producing 300,000 each day. If you're wondering about the origins of the name *yo-yo*, in the Filipino language, it means to come back.

Philippine Immigrants

After the Spanish-American War, the United States paid Spain $20 million for the Philippines. It would remain under American control for nearly fifty years. During that time, thousands of young *Filipinos* (men) enrolled in American universities, while a great many others sought work on the Hawaiian sugar plantations. Searching for better work, many migrated to Washington, California, and Alaska.

Some *Filipinas* (women) came to the United States after World War II as wives of the American servicemen who had been stationed in the Philippines. In the 1960s, many more would come to the states as nurses, filling an ongoing shortage in American hospitals.

Make Your Own Yo-Yo

You can do all kinds of tricks with yo-yos. But there is a trick or two to making them—like twisting and attaching the string the right way. Here are some tips for crafting a yo-yo of your own and then taking it for a spin.

WHAT YOU NEED

- **Thin wooden circles, one ³/₄ inch in diameter and two 2 ¹/₈ inches in diameter (sold in craft supply stores)**
- **Tacky glue or wood glue**
- **Assorted buttons (optional)**
- **Measuring tape**
- **Scissors**
- **Thin cotton string**
- **Duct tape**
- **Paper clip**

WHAT YOU DO

1 Glue the small circle to the center of 1 large circle. Glue the remaining circle on top, aligning the edges of the larger circles. Let the glue dry.

2 Glue on buttons for decoration.

3 Have a friend measure the distance from your elbow to the floor. Cut string 2 times this length. Tape one end of the string to the back of a chair.

4 Bend a paper clip as shown and tie the loose string end to the hook. Hold the straightened end of the clip and back away from the chair until the string is taut.

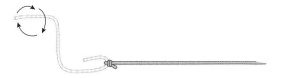

5 Crank the string clockwise until it is tight (it can take up to 500 turns). Ask a friend to hold the middle while you bring the two ends together. Remove the paper clip and the tape. Release the middle and let the line twist around itself. Stretch out the line. This is your yo-yo string.

6 Tie a finger-size loop at the top of the string (where you brought the ends together). Attach the end to the yo-yo by separating the strands and looping one strand around the center circle. Twist the string a few times to tighten the loop. Wind up your yo-yo and give it a whirl.

Bluegrass Banjo

With a box and a few other household items, you can build a simple banjo that really plays. At the same time, you will learn about the science of music by hearing how the size of the rubber-band strings affects the pitch.

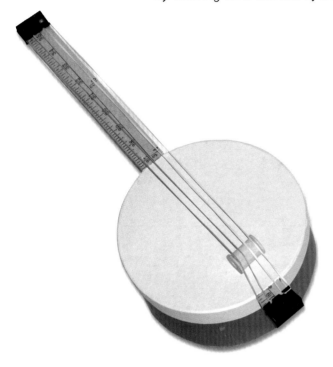

- ❖ **Handsaw**
- ❖ **Craft knife**
- ❖ **2 large binder clips**
- ❖ **Double-sided tape**
- ❖ **2 rubber bands**
- ❖ **Wooden thread spool**

WHAT YOU DO

1 Remove box lid and set it aside. Measure the height of the box and write that down. Measure the circumference (around the outside) of the box and write that down. Cut a piece of decorative paper as long as the circumference and as high as the box's height. Glue paper around box.

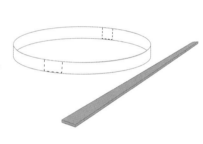

WHAT YOU NEED

- ❖ **Round paper box and lid (sold in craft supply stores)**
- ❖ **Measuring tape**
- ❖ **Pencil and paper**
- ❖ **Scissors**
- ❖ **Scrapbook or decorative paper**
- ❖ **Glue stick**
- ❖ **Yardstick**

2 Saw the yardstick in half. Ask a grownup for help or permission to use the saw. Cut a pair of notches (just wide enough for the yardstick to fit into) on opposite sides of the box lid's rim.

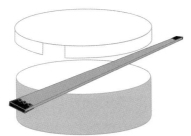

3 Attach the binder clips to the yardstick ends. Then remove the clip handles by pinching the sides together and sliding the ends out of their channels.

4 Set the box, open side down, on a table. Place the yardstick on top and push the box lid down over the box bottom, aligning the notches over the stick. Use double-sided tape to secure the cover in place.

5 Stretch the rubber bands between the binder clips, slipping the ends over the clips' curved edges.

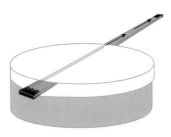

6 Fit the thread spool under the rubber band near the bottom of the yardstick and your banjo is ready to pluck or strum. If it doesn't make a good sound, try using thinner or shorter rubber bands. This will raise the pitch because smaller bands will vibrate faster, and the faster the vibration, the higher the tone.

Here's The Story

In pre–Civil War America, African Americans took pleasure in strumming the banjo. They used large, hollowed-out gourds to make their instruments, modeling them after those they had played in Africa. Later, when African Americans went to work in the Appalachian coal mines, the Irish and Scottish immigrants adopted the banjo as their own.

Woolen Toys

When it came to making clothes in Colonial America, early settlers had to be resourceful. They raised sheep so they could spin the wool into yarn for knitting sweaters and stockings and to weave cloth for sewing other kinds of clothes. Even the leftover bits of yarn were turned into little dolls for children. Making yarn dolls remained a popular pastime among settlers moving across the prairie. Not only were they fun to play with, they were also used to decorate Christmas trees.

In time, the American flocks grew large enough to produce a surplus of wool that could be shipped to other countries in trade for goods the colonists wanted to import. When Great Britain caught wind of this, it quickly passed the Woolen Act of 1699, which forbade the colonists from exporting any of their wool and pretty much anything they made from it.

Braided Octopus

As simple as they are, old-fashioned yarn dolls have plenty of personality. Add a new twist to the traditional technique, and you can wind up with a pair of extra-colorful underwater characters.

WHAT YOU NEED

- ❖ **Yarn**
- ❖ **Cardboard, 9 inches high**
- ❖ **Scissors**
- ❖ **Rubber bands**
- ❖ **Googly eyes**
- ❖ **Craft glue**

WHAT YOU DO

1 Wrap yarn around the cardboard 50 times. Cut the yarn and slide the bunched coils (called a *hank*) off the cardboard.

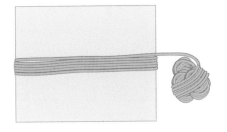

2 Thread a short piece of yarn through the top of the hank and tie it tightly. Cut the strands at the bottom of the hank so they hang free. Set aside.

3 Wind more yarn into a 2-inch ball. Slip the ball inside the top of the hank, right under the tie. Arrange the strands evenly, and, with another piece of yarn, tie around the whole bunch right under the ball.

4 Divide the strands below the head into 8 sections. Wrap rubber bands around each section until you're ready for them.

5 For each section, remove the rubber band, braid the section, then put the rubber band back on. Fold a 6-inch piece of yarn in half and lay it on top of the rubber band.

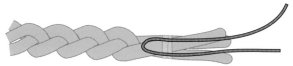

6 Wind one of the hanging strands snugly around it, working your way toward the loop.

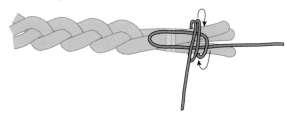

7 Thread the end through the loop and pull on the other hanging strand until the loop slides under the wound yarn.

8 Repeat for each of the other sections. Trim the ends evenly below the wound yarn.

9 Glue a pair of large googly eyes to the yarn near the base of the head.

Leggy Red Crab

WHAT YOU NEED

- ❖ **Yarn**
- ❖ **Cardboard, 9-inches high**
- ❖ **Scissors**
- ❖ **Rubber bands**
- ❖ **Googly eyes**
- ❖ **Craft glue**

WHAT YOU DO

1 Wrap yarn around the cardboard 50 times. Cut the yarn and slide the bunched coils, or hank, off the cardboard (see p. 90, step 1).

2 Cut a 2-inch piece of yarn and thread it through the top of the hank and tie it tightly. Tie the bottom of the hank in the same manner.

3 To form the head, wind more yarn into a 1½-inch ball. Slip the ball into the middle of the hank. Cut 2 pieces of yarn about 2 inches each and use them to tie the hank on both sides of the head.

4 Cut the strands at both ends of the hank and divide each section into 2 groups. Tie around each group right below the ties you made in step 3.

5 Use the front group on each side to make a claw. Tie 2 pieces of yarn around the upper claw to create joints, spaced about ½ inch apart. Split the strands below the joints into 2 sections for the pincers, making one bigger than the other.

6 Fold a 10-inch piece of yarn in half and lay it on top of a pincer.

7 Wind one of the hanging strands snugly around the pincer, working your way toward the loop.

8 Thread the end through the loop and pull on the other hanging strand until the loop slides under the wound yarn.

9 Wrap the remaining three pincers with yarn in the same way.

10 Divide the remaining strands on each side of the crab into 4 groups. Braid each group to create a leg, and secure the end with a rubber band. Then use a 6-inch piece of yarn to wrap the leg end as you did the pincers.

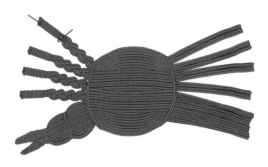

11 For eyestalks, gather six 4-inch strands of yarn and tie an overhand knot at the top

of the bunch. Braid the strands and end with another overhand knot.

12 Use your finger to separate a few strands at the front of the crab's head and thread the eyestalk braid through so that it sticks out about 1 inch onboth ends.

13 Glue small googly eyes to the ends of the stalks.

So What's a Hank?

A coil or skein of yarn is called a *hank*.

Navajo Weaving

One of the most prized arts to come from the American Southwest is the bold, colorful weaving done by the women of the Navajo tribe. The Navajo learned weaving from the Pueblos, who had learned how to weave striped patterns from the Spanish.

The Navajos, rather than always weaving strands of wool all the way across the loom, would change direction, thereby creating diagonal lines called *lazy-lines*. This allowed the Navajo to weave zigzags and diamonds into their designs. These unique patterns, plus the fact that the weave was tight enough to shed water, make Navajo blankets treasured items.

By the late 1880s, Native American art had become collectors' items. Navajo weavers began making thicker, heavier blankets that were used as rugs and today are highly prized.

Tiny Tapestries

With a simple cardboard loom, you can design your own miniature Navajo-style weaving to use as a dollhouse rug or a coaster for a cup of hot cocoa.

WHAT YOU NEED

- ❖ **4½ x 6-inch piece of thin cardboard**
- ❖ **Ruler**
- ❖ **Scissors**
- ❖ **Yarn**
- ❖ **Plastic darning needle**
- ❖ **Wooden craft (popsicle) stick**
- ❖ **A few beads**

Threading the Loom

Keep in mind that the string passes twice through all of the top notches but only once through the bottom notches (with the exception of the last notch).

WHAT YOU DO

1 Along both shorter sides of the cardboard, cut ¼-inch-deep notches every ¼ inch. Turn your cardboard loom so these notches are at top and bottom.

2 With the yarn still on the skein, measure 4 inches of yarn and thread it through the first notch in the top left. Wrap the yarn around the back of the loom and

through the first notch in the bottom left. Bring the yarn up the front and thread it back through the first notch in the top left.

3 Bring the yarn across the back of the loom and through the second top notch, then down the front into the second bottom notch. Bring the yarn across the back and through the third notch on the bottom. Bring the yarn up the front and through the fourth top notch.

4 Continue this pattern, working all the way to the right. After threading the yarn through the last notch, loop the yarn down the back of the loom one more time. End by coming through the bottom right corner and leaving a 4-inch tail.

5 Now that you have the warp threads in place (the ones you will weave around), you're ready to start weaving. Thread the needle with a 24-inch piece of yarn.

6 Start on the right, an inch or so from the bottom, and weave the craft stick over and then under the warp threads. Slide the threaded needle through the separated threads below the stick. When you reach the left side, slide the craft stick down, pushing the yarn all the way to the bottom of the loom.

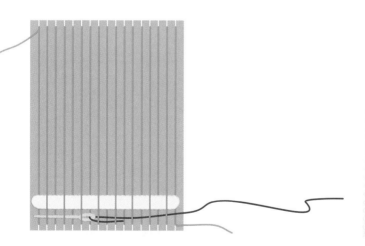

7 Remove the craft stick. Reinsert the craft stick, but this time going under, then over the warp threads. Slide the needle back through the threads to the right. Be careful not to pull the yarn too tightly or the tapestry will curve in on the sides. Slide the craft stick down again to push the second row close against the first. Continue weaving back and forth, changing colors as you like, until you've filled the loom.

8 Remove the tapestry from the loom. Use the needle to weave a new thread along each of the 4 edges. Use the ends to tie a tassel at each corner. (Unlike other styles, Navajo weaving isn't fringed along the entire edge). Lastly, weave any loose yarn ends into the tapestry.

Threading on More Yarn

For the best results, add new strands of yarn at the beginning or end of a row.

Lazy-Lines Designs

Weaving a design with Navajo-style lazy lines is easy. To create a diamond, the first row of weaving should wrap around 1 warp thread and the row above it around 2, then around 3, and so on until you reach the center of your diamond. Then decrease the number of warp strings by 1 in each of the following rows. When you have finished, use a different color of yarn to fill in the area around the diamond.

Drawstring Purse

You can also use your loom to make a small pouch or drawstring purse. Weave all the way around the cardboard instead of going back and forth across the front. Push your first rows as far down the loom as possible so the rows at the bottom of the purse will be tight against each other. When you have finished weaving, bend the tabs at the top of the loom and slide the purse off the cardboard. Then weave a long doubled thread for a drawstring around the top and tie beads on the ends to keep them from pulling through.

Cowboy Braids

Try your hand at a classic cowboy craft by braiding a decorative leather dangler for your key chain or backpack. Horse tack shops often sell inexpensive bags of assorted leather strips and laces that are perfect for this. Here's how you can create two different styles of flat braids. On page 100, you'll find directions for making a square braid.

WHAT YOU DO

1 To create a braid like the dark brown one on the left, attach 2 leather laces to the key chain ring with a lark's head knot. Follow the step-by-step diagrams below.

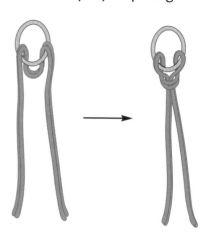

2 Separate the laces as shown.

1   2 3   4

WHAT YOU NEED

❖ **Leather laces or rawhide shoelaces, each about 24 inches long**

❖ **Scissors**

❖ **Key chain ring**

3 Beginning at the left side, cross the first strand over the second. Cross the third strand over the fourth. Then cross the new third strand over the new second strand.

4 Continue this way, stopping 1½ inches from the ends of the leather strands.

5 Cut an 8-inch length of leather lace. Fold it in half and lay it on top of the end.

6 Wind one of the hanging strands snugly around it, working your way toward the loop. Thread the end through it.

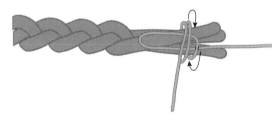

7 Pull on the other hanging strand until the loop slides under the wound strands.

HERE'S ANOTHER WAY

1 To create a braid like the light brown one in the picture, attach 2 leather laces of the same length to the key chain ring using a lark's head knot as in step 1 on opposite page. Arrange the strands side by side.

2 Starting on the far left, cross the first lace over the middle two laces. Then cross the fourth lace over the new pair of middle strands. Continue in this way until you're near the end. Tie off the braid as in steps 5, 6, and 7 in the first key chain.

Giddyup!

Square Braid

WHAT YOU NEED

- **Leather laces or rawhide shoelaces, each about 24 inches long**
- **Scissors**
- **Key chain ring**

WHAT YOU DO

1 Attach two 24-inch leather laces to the key chain ring using a lark's head knot, as described for the flat braid on page 98 (step 1).

2 Spread the 4 hanging strips apart to form an X. The ring should be underneath the laces.

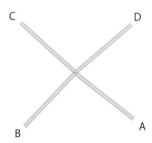

3 Start braiding counterclockwise: place strand A over D.

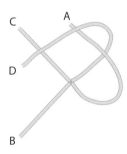

4 Next, lay strand D over A and C.

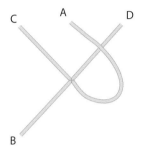

5 Then bring strand C over D and B.

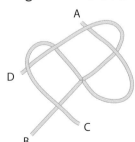

6 Finally, weave strand B over C and through the loop formed by A.

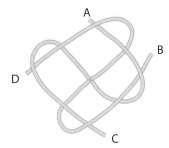

7 Pull all of the strings equally to tighten the knot.

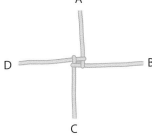

8 Tie a second knot as you did the first, except this time work clockwise. Continue tying knots, switching directions each time and stopping about 1½ inches from the ends of the leather laces.

9 To finish, use an 8-inch length of leather lace and follow steps 5, 6, and 7 on page 99.

Here's The Story

You may have seen movies about the Old West featuring rough-riding American cowboys driving cattle across the plains. By the time the first English-speaking settlers headed west in the 1800s, there were plenty of cattle to round up—millions, in fact—and there were skilled cowboys from Mexico, called *vaqueros*, to lead the way. The *vaqueros* had learned their skills from the Spanish, who had brought cows to Mexico nearly three hundred years earlier.

Driving cattle across the open plains following the spring roundup was no easy feat. For starters, the drive could last for months, and it didn't take much to panic a herd. Sometimes a mere sneeze was enough to start a stampede.

As the *vaqueros* gained experience, they invented new items to make their lives easier and more comfortable, such as lassos, chaps, and ponchos. They also became expert at repairing bridles, lines, and other leather gear. By sharing what they knew, you could say the *vaqueros* blazed a trail for the American cowboys to follow.

Yarn Painting

To "spin a yarn" is an expression that means to tell a story—and that's exactly what you can do with this craft. Think of a simple image to sketch of something you like. Color it in with yarn, and you will have a picture that's worth a thousand words.

WHAT YOU NEED

❖ **Piece of wood or cardboard to use as a canvas**
❖ **Pencil**
❖ **Yarn**
❖ **Scissors**
❖ **White glue**
❖ **Paintbrush**
❖ **Toothpick**

WHAT YOU DO

1 Sketch a design on the wood or cardboard.

2 Choose a shape within your design to begin with and cut a long piece of the color yarn you want to fill it in with.

3 Use the paintbrush to spread glue along the outline, lay the yarn on top, and press down gently with your fingertips. Apply more glue and yarn, working your way into the center of the shape. Use a toothpick to move the yarn, if necessary. Continue in this way until the whole canvas is filled.

Choosing the Right Yarn

Different types of yarns will create various effects. Cotton yarns, for example, are good for creating animals with smooth, distinct lines, while wools and acrylics produce fuzzy animals.

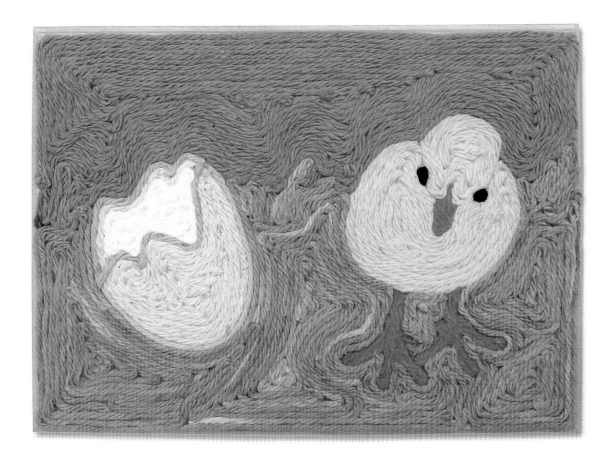

Here's The Story

The arrival of the Spanish settlers in Mexico in the 1500s greatly influenced many of the native people who lived there. The Huichol Indians were different. Because their villages were isolated in the Sierra Madres Mountains, they were able to hold onto their pre-Columbus way of life.

The Huichols hold a deep respect for nature and believe that people, plants, and all elements of the universe are equally important. These beliefs are reflected in their detailed and imaginative artwork. One of their most distinctive crafts is yarn painting. In their paintings, the Huichols cover circles or squares of wood with beeswax and then press on colorful strands of yarn to create meaningful symbols or images.

Fabric, Felt, and Fleece

Long before the word "sampler" was used to describe a box of assorted chocolates, it referred to a long strip of linen embroidered with letters and numbers. In Colonial America, samplers of this sort were often sewn by young schoolgirls learning the art of needlework. It wasn't unusual for a finished piece to contain a mistake or two. In time, though, samplers became an art. Designed to be framed, they typically featured verses or whole poems composed by the embroiderer.

Like the linen on which these early samplers were sewn, lots of different fabrics have served as canvases for artistic expression. The following projects are inspired by some of the innovative techniques—quilting, dyeing, and felting, to name a few—that were developed by textile artists around the world and then found their way to America.

FeLT FaShions

Just how felt was invented is a fascinating story. Well, actually there is more than one story. Some say it happened by accident when someone in China used wool to pad under a horse's saddle only to have friction between the leather and the animal's sweaty hide turn the fleece into thick, matted cloth. Others claim it was discovered underfoot by a European pilgrim who lined his sandals with wool. Still another tale credits an Asian shepherd's dog for sleeping on top of a pile of wool.

No matter where felt first came from, it was destined to become a valuable material worldwide. In the 1600s, Dutch and British colonies in America sent beaver pelts to Europe where they could be "felted" for making hats. It wasn't long, though, before the colonists had a booming felt hat business of their own. When Britain found out what her colonies were up to, it passed the Hat Act of 1732, which forbade American colonists from selling their felt wares to anyone but each other. Today, of course, felt is available to everyone. On the following pages are directions to help you make a lovely felt purse.

Flowery Felt Purse

What's especially fun about this lightweight shoulder bag is that the felt flowers button on and off. That means you can cut out a whole bouquet of different colors and styles to pick and choose whatever strikes your fancy.

WHAT YOU NEED

- ❖ **18 x 7½-inch felt rectangle**
- ❖ **Ruler**
- ❖ **Chalk**
- ❖ **Needle and thread**
- ❖ **Buttons**
- ❖ **Fabric glue**
- ❖ **Fabric scissors**
- ❖ **Yarn**
- ❖ **Straight pins**
- ❖ **Colored felt scraps for flowers**
- ❖ **Self-sticking Velcro fastener**

WHAT YOU DO

1 Place the felt rectangle on a flat surface with the shorter edges at the top and bottom. Use the ruler and chalk to mark a horizontal line 7½ inches from the bottom and another line 3 inches from the top. Fold the bottom of the felt along the lower line, and fold down the top of the felt along the upper line. This is what the purse will look like when it is closed.

2 Mark a few chalk spots on the purse where you'd like to add felt flowers. Then unfold the felt and sew buttons on those spots.

3 From the top chalk line down, run a line of fabric glue along the sides of the purse. Fold the bottom of the felt to the chalk line, and press the side edges together. Set the purse aside to dry.

4 Cut about eighteen 4-foot strands of yarn for the shoulder strap. Using an overhand knot, tie the yarn strands together 1 inch from one of the ends. Braid the strands, stopping 1 inch from the ends. Tie a second knot to secure the ends.

5 Place 1 knot at each of the bottom corners and pin the braid up against the glued sides. Sew the strap in place. Leave the upper flap free.

6 For each flower, cut out a felt circle (about 3 inches across for a larger blossom and 2 inches across for a smaller one). Trim the edge to look like petals. Cut a buttonhole in the middle of the circles and slip each over one of the buttons. For a flower center, cut out a smaller circle in a contrasting color and attach it the same way.

7 Stick a Velcro fastener to the underside of the flap to keep it closed.

Food for Thought

If you like cookies, you can thank the Dutch immigrants for making them popular in America. As a special holiday treat, they would make tasty little cakes called *koekjes* by rolling out sweet dough, pressing it with carved wooden molds, and then baking the decorative

Dutch Immigrants

Dutch fur traders came to America in the early 1600s looking for otter and beaver skins to sell to the Europeans. They set up trading posts and formed the Dutch West India Company and paid Dutch farm families to settle in the area. These early colonists ended up living on an island, which they called New Amsterdam. Today that island is known as Manhattan.

The houses that the Dutch colonists built in America resembled the homes they left in the Netherlands, with stone walls and gambrel roofs for more attic space. If you think of an ordinary straight roof looking like the letter V turned upside down, you could say a gambrel roof resembles an inverted U. Dutch houses also had doors that were cut in half. That way you could open the top to let in fresh air and leave the bottom closed to keep animals out.

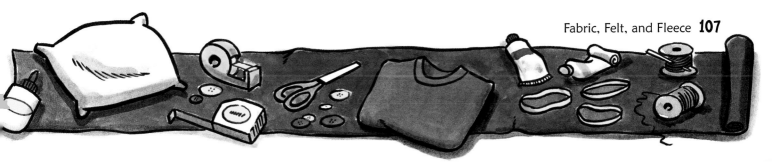

Appliqué

Before the American Civil War, African American women were often trained to be seamstresses and quilt makers. A favored technique was appliqué, in which fabric shapes were sewn on top of another layer of cloth.

One of these women was Harriet Powers, who came to be known as the mother of African American quilting. Although Harriet could not read or write, she learned the stories of the Bible from singing spirituals and listening to sermons. One of her most famous works consists of eleven panels that illustrate the Biblical story of how the animals got their names. Among the creatures she appliquéd are an elephant, an ostrich, a salamander, and three camels. Besides portraying Biblical tales, Harriet's work also recorded historical events, such as an extraordinary meteor shower that took place in 1833.

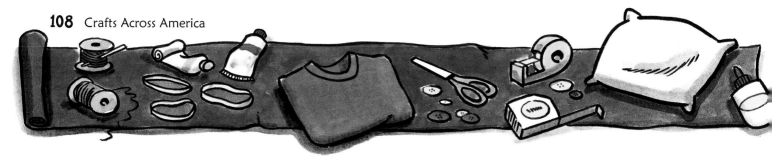

Build-a-House Pillow Top

Appliqué is like a collage, but instead of cutting the pieces out of paper, you snip them from colorful cloth. For your first design, stick with basic shapes that will be easy and quick to sew. You can build a house, for example, out of a rectangle topped with square windows and a triangle roof. This design would make a great design for a throw pillow.

WHAT YOU NEED

❖ **13 x 17-inch cotton fabric for the pillow front**

❖ **13 x 23-inch cotton fabric for the pillow back**

❖ **Scraps of assorted cotton fabric**

❖ **Pencil**

❖ **Construction paper**

❖ **Scissors**

❖ **Measuring tape**

❖ **Chalk**

❖ **Fabric scissors**

❖ **Straight pins**

❖ **Thread and sewing needle**

❖ **Measuring tape**

❖ **12 x 16-inch pillow**

WHAT YOU DO

1 Wash and dry the fabric so it will not shrink later.

2 Sketch the pieces of your design on construction paper. Cut them out and arrange them on the pillow front to see how they will fit. Lay the cutouts on the fabric and draw around them with chalk. Cut out the pieces, adding a 1/4-inch seam allowance all the way around each piece.

3 On the first piece, turn under the border so the chalk line doesn't show and pinch the folds. Pin the finger-pressed piece in place.

4 Thread your needle with a single 24-inch length of thread. Knot the end. Poke the needle up through the wrong side of the piece close to the edge and then back down through the pillow front. Continue sewing all the way around the piece.

5 Continue pinning and sewing the rest of the pieces.

6 To finish the pillow cover, cut the fabric for the back into two 13 x 11½-inch pieces. On each piece, fold the cut edge under ½ inch and press it with the iron. Ask a grownup for

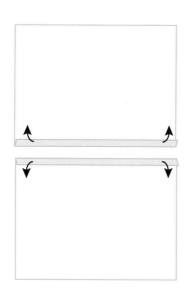

help or permission to use the iron. Fold over another ½ inch and press it with the iron again. Stitch the pressed edges in place.

7 Pin the 2 pieces, right side down, on top of your pillow top, matching up the outer edges and overlapping the sewn edges by 2 inches. Stitch around both pieces ½ inch from the outer edges and leaving the overlapped seams unstitched.

Cutting Cloth

To keep your fabric scissors sharp, don't use them to cut anything but material, not even paper, and especially not cardboard.

8 Trim the fabric diagonally at the corners. Turn the cover right side out. Stuff your pillow inside.

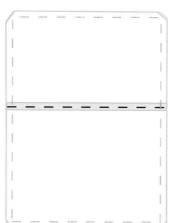

Japanese Jigsaw

Turning one hundred years old is a big deal. When that day came for America, in 1876, it was only fitting that Philadelphia, the city where the Declaration of Independence was signed, would host the first major World's Fair held in the United States.

One of the most popular attractions at the fair was the Japanese exhibit, which featured an unusual kind of pottery. Its glaze was covered with tiny cracks called *crazing*. When American quilters saw it, they were eager to recreate the effect in cloth and started piecing together bits of silk, velvet, and other fabric scraps, any which way. When it came to choosing colors, they decided anything would go. In no time, these fanciful new quilts, called *crazies*, were all the rage.

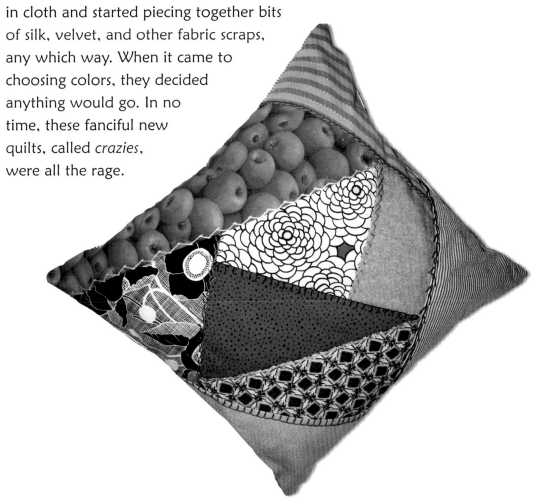

Crazy Quilt Pillow

It doesn't take much fabric, or time, to piece together a crazy quilt square big enough to cover a throw pillow, especially if you use what's called the "sew and flip" technique. This is a great way to turn swatches from your favorite worn-out clothes into a colorful keepsake. Or you can check out the remnant bin at the fabric store and choose pieces in your best friend's favorite color to make her a gift she is sure to be crazy about.

WHAT YOU NEED

- ❖ **Assorted cotton fabric scraps**
- ❖ **16-inch square of muslin fabric**
- ❖ **Fabric scissors**
- ❖ **Straight pins**
- ❖ **Thread and sewing needle**
- ❖ **16 x 22-inch piece of cotton fabric for the pillow back**
- ❖ **Embroidery floss and embroidery needle**
- ❖ **Measuring tape**
- ❖ **Iron**
- ❖ **15-inch square pillow**

WHAT YOU DO

1 Wash and dry all the fabric pieces. Cut a fabric scrap to start with and place it right side up in the center of the muslin. Place a second scrap face down on top of the first, matching both along 1 edge. Pin both pieces in place.

2 Thread the sewing needle and sew the pieces to the muslin with a line of short, even stitches 1/4 inch from the common edge. Knot and trim the thread end and remove the pins.

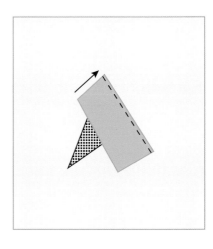

3 Flip over the top piece of fabric. Smooth the seam with your fingertips to flatten it.

4 Choose another fabric scrap and pin it, right side down, on top of the first 2 pieces, matching 1 of its edges to an edge formed by the 2 joined pieces. Sew the pieces to the muslin as before, then flip over the new piece.

5 Continue adding pieces this way until all of the muslin is covered. Sew around the square, ¼ inch from the edges to hold all the layers together.

6 Use some of the fancy embroidery stitches shown below to stitch around each of the crazy pieces.

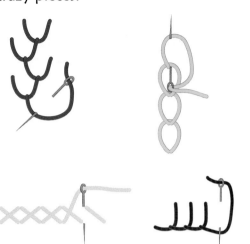

7 To finish your pillow, follow steps 6, 7, and 8 of the Appliqué Pillow on page 110.

Silky Slip Covers

After you have mastered the crazy quilting technique, try collecting old silk ties that your father or grandfather is going to throw away. Use this silk to make a lovely pillow.

Frilly Flowers

Here's The Story

In the mid 1800s, an Ohio doctor and politician named Levi L. Lamborn imported six carnation seedlings from France. Under his care, one of the seedlings produced a frilly scarlet blossom. It was the first carnation to bloom in America. Lamborn proudly presented it to his friend and political rival William McKinley to wear in his lapel. McKinley considered the carnation good luck and, in fact, went on to become the twenty-fifth president of the United States. The scarlet carnation was destined for success too. It became the state flower of Ohio, and Lamborn's hometown of Alliance was named Carnation City of the United States.

CLOTh CarnaTions

Say the word carnation *and the picture of a ruffled red, pink, or white blossom is likely to pop into your mind. Actually, carnations come in just about any color except blue. Grow your own variety of flowers out of fabric: checks, stripes, prints, polka-dots, and even blue. With these flowers, anything goes.*

WHAT YOU NEED

- ❖ **Thin craft or floral wire**
- ❖ **Wire cutters**
- ❖ **Measuring tape**
- ❖ **Fabric scissors**
- ❖ **Lightweight fabric scraps**
- ❖ **Paper clip**

WHAT YOU DO

1 Cut a piece of wire double the length of the stem you want. Bend the wire in half.

2 For each flower, cut six 2½ by 3-inch pieces of fabric. If you're working with cotton, you can fringe the edges of the material by pulling several of the outer threads from the weave to give your flower an extra-frilly look.

3 Stack the 6 pieces of fabric on top of each other.

4 Starting at one of the 3-inch edges of the fabric stack, fold the bunch as you would a paper fan, making the pleats about ½ inch wide.

5 Sandwich the folded fabric between the bend in the wire. Twist the wire ends together. The tighter you twist the wires, the stronger the stem will be.

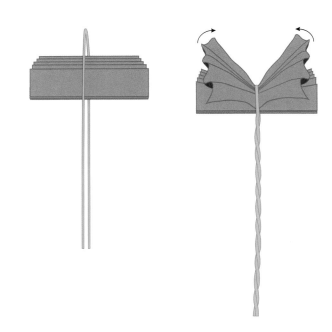

6 Separate the layers of fabric, pulling them up toward the center to shape a bushy carnation.

Tie-Dye T's

Here's The Story

During the 1960s, when the United States first established the Peace Corps, young American volunteers were sent to Africa to help build schools and hospitals. The Africans taught them a method of knotting and dyeing cloth to create bold and vibrant designs. When they went home, the Americans brought the technique with them, and tie-dye caught on immediately.

Circles of Color

Tie-dye is one fashion that never seems to be out of style. In fact, you can create all kinds of unique and interesting effects. The following method creates bright bursts of color.

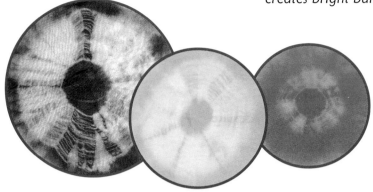

WHAT YOU NEED

- ❖ **Cotton T-shirt, prewashed and dried**
- ❖ **Pennies or other coins**
- ❖ **Lots of rubber bands**
- ❖ **Fabric dye (such as Rit brand liquid or powder dye) of different colors**
- ❖ **Salt**
- ❖ **Large pots or other containers for mixing the dye baths (as specified by the dye manufacturer's directions)**
- ❖ **Rubber gloves**
- ❖ **Kitchen tongs**
- ❖ **Source of running water for rinsing**

WHAT YOU DO

1 Push a penny against the fabric from the underside. Gather the fabric around it and bind tightly with a rubber band just below

the coin. Bind the fabric with a couple more rubber bands below the first and spaced an inch or so apart. Repeat this with several more coins.

2 Mix 2 or more dye baths according to manufacturer's directions. Wear rubber gloves to protect your hands.

3 Use kitchen tongs to dip your shirt in the dye for a couple of minutes or so. (Follow the manufacturer's directions for times.) You can either dip the bound portions individually in different colors or submerge the whole garment in one color.

4 Rinse the dyed shirt under cold running water until the water runs clear. Remove the rubber bands and coins and rinse again.

5 Gently squeeze out water and hang up the shirt to dry.

Striped Tie-Dyed Tank

To create a unique pattern of multi-colored stripes, try this folding method.

1 Fold the entire shirt accordion-style and then fold the whole thing in half. Bind the fabric every inch or so with rubber bands.

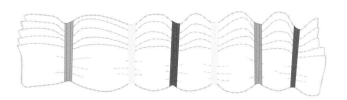

2 Mix 2 dye baths (1 red and 1 blue) according to the manufacturer's directions. Wear rubber gloves to protect your hands.

3 Use kitchen tongs to dip ⅔ of the accordion-folded shirt in red dye for a couple of minutes or so. (Follow manufacturer's directions for specific times.) Turn it around and dip ⅔ in blue dye. This will create a deep purple band where the colors overlap.

4 Rinse the dyed shirt under cold running water until the water runs clear. Remove rubber bands and rinse the shirt again.

5 Gently squeeze out water and hang up the shirt to dry.

CRAFT HINT

Laundering Your New T

Always wash your tie-dyed shirt separately in case the dye bleeds.

ALL Sew'n Up

Another interesting technique involves stitching a series of lines in the fabric as below. The result is uneven stripes cascading down the shirt.

1 Begin by stitching a series of lines in the fabric using strong nylon thread or dental floss.

2 Gather the material by pulling the threads and tightly knotting the thread ends together.

3 Mix the dye baths according to the manufacturer's directions. Wear rubber gloves to protect your hands.

4 Soak the fabric in lukewarm water for a few minutes. Then transfer to the dye bath for 15 to 20 minutes.

5 Rinse the dyed shirt under cold running water until the water runs clear. Remove the threads, being careful not to snip the fabric of the shirt. Rinse the shirt again.

6 Gently squeeze out water and hang up the shirt to dry.

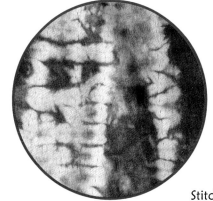

Stitched pattern close-up

Batik Wall Art

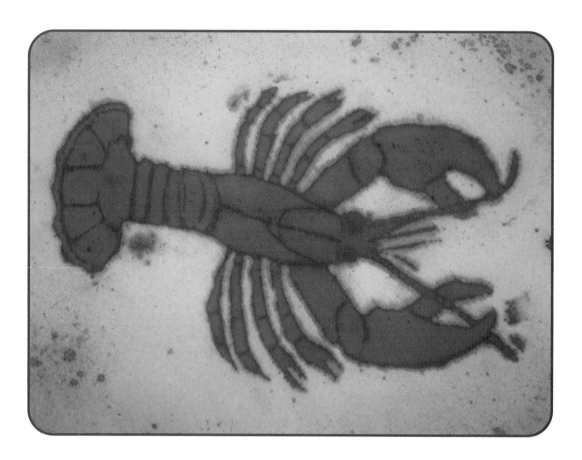

Here's The Story

Some 17,500 tropical islands make up Indonesia, and one of the biggest islands is Java. For centuries, the Javanese have created beautiful designs on cloth by using a special tool called a *tjanting* to drip hot wax on the material before they dye it. This process is called *batik*. The wax blocks the dye so that only the cloth around it changes color.

In the 1700s, during the time Indonesia was a Dutch colony, traders discovered batik and introduced it to Europe. But it would be another 200 years or so before the art found its way to the United States. Once it did, though, batik became fashionable, particularly during the 1960s.

Spray-Dyed Wall Hanging

Instead of using hot wax to create batik, use white glue brushed onto fabric. Once the glue dries, it will resist the dye. When you are finished, wash the glue out with water. Small spray bottles come in handy for applying color quickly and easily, as do fabric pens for adding fine detail.

WHAT YOU NEED

- ❖ **Fabric scissors**
- ❖ **Muslin**
- ❖ **Pencil**
- ❖ **Wax paper**
- ❖ **Glue and a small container to pour it into**
- ❖ **Small, stiff paintbrush**
- ❖ **Wire baking rack**
- ❖ **Fabric dye, prepared according to the manufacturer's directions**
- ❖ **Rubber gloves**
- ❖ **Kitchen funnel and small spray bottles**
- ❖ **Running water**
- ❖ **Fabric pens**
- ❖ **Wooden dowel**
- ❖ **Yarn**

WHAT YOU DO

1 Trim a piece of muslin to the size you want. Lightly sketch or trace an image onto it.

2 Place the muslin on a sheet of wax paper. Paint glue over any parts of the design you do *not* want to dye. It may be part of the image, such as the petals of a daisy, or you can paint glue around an entire image you'd like to tint. Apply enough glue to soak through the fabric. Set the muslin on the wire rack to dry.

3 Prepare dye and pour it into small spray bottles. With rubber gloves on and working outdoors or over a sink, spray the nonglued sections of your design with dye.

4 After the dye is dry, rinse the glue out with cool running water, using your fingers to gently rub it away. Let muslin dry.

5 Use fabric pens to outline your design or to add detail. You can spritz more dye to create an interesting background.

6 Glue the top edge of the muslin to a wooden dowel. Tie yarn to the ends of the dowel, and hang your batik.

Glossary

appliqué Needlework in which cut pieces of fabric are sewn onto a larger piece of fabric.

circumference The distance around something.

construction paper A type of colored, heavyweight paper that is often used for craft or school projects.

cotton batting A dense, soft layer of cotton that is often used to stuff quilts.

craft or floral wire A thin, soft wire that bends easily and can be easily cut and used to hold flowers in place in bouquets.

craft scissors Special scissors that will make decorative edges when used; they come in many different designs.

doubloon A Spanish gold coin from centuries in the past.

embroidery needle A needle with a very long eye and made to hold thicker thread.

embroidery floss Cotton thread made up of 6 strands which can be separated.

fabric scissors Large scissors or shears that are especially made for cutting fabric.

fishing swivel A small mechanism used with fishing line and having a middle part that will revolve and with a circle on each end.

medicine man Among Native Americans, a man thought to have magical healing powers.

mulberry paper A paper with a handmade look that is often used in scrapbooks.

muslin fabric Lightweight cotton cloth in a plain, tight weave.

overhand knot This is a simple knot that most people use to tie their shoelaces.

Peace Corps A government agency, formed during the 1960s, that sent Americans to foreign countries to teach farming, business, and other ways to help the native people.

pinking shears Special scissors that cut zigzag edges to prevent raveling.

sampler A piece of needlework worked with a variety of stitches meant to show the skill of the seamstress.

tamale wrappers Specially prepared cornhusk used for food. Can be bought in most grocery stores.

wooden dowel A thin, round stick that comes in various lengths.

Index

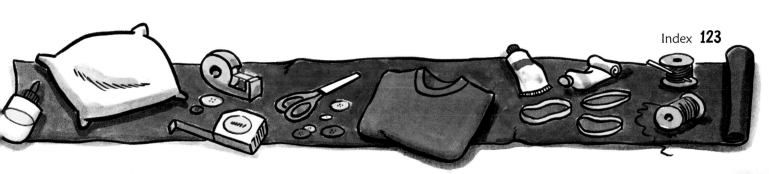

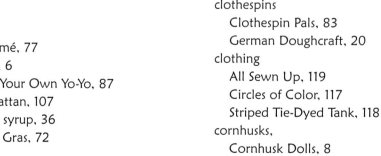

More Good Books from Williamson Books

Williamson Books are available from your bookseller or directly from Ideals Publications.
Please see last page for ordering information or to visit our website.

Kids Can!® Books for Ages 7 to 14

Leap into Space!
Exploring the Universe
and Your Place in It
BY NANCY F. CASTALDO

Super Science Concoctions
50 Mysterious Mixtures
for Fabulous Fun
BY JILL FRANKEL HAUSER

Parents' Choice Recommended
Making Amazing Art!
40 Activities Using the 7
Elements of Art Design
BY SANDI HENRY

**The Kids' Multicultural
Art Book**
Art & Craft Experiences
from Around the World
BY ALEXANDRA MICHAELS

Parents' Choice Approved
*Skipping Stones Multicultural
    Honor Award*
*Benjamin Franklin Best Multicultural
    Book Award*
**The Kids'
Multicultural Cookbook**
Food & Fun Around
the World
BY DEANNA F. COOK

Parents' Choice Approved
**The Kids' Multicultural
Craft Book**
35 Crafts from Around the
World
BY ROBERTA GOULD

American Bookseller Pick of the Lists
Dr. Toy Best Vacation Product
**Kids' Crazy Art
Concoctions**
50 Mysterious Mixtures
for Art & Craft Fun
BY JILL FRANKEL HAUSER

Parent's Guide Children's Media Award
Kids' Art Works!
Creating with Color,
Design, Texture & More
BY SANDI HENRY

American Bookseller Pick of the List
Oppenheim Toy Portfolio Best Book Award
*Skipping Stones Nature & Ecology Honor
    Award*
EcoArt!
Earth-Friendly Art &
Craft Experiences for
3- to 9-Year-Olds
BY LAURIE CARLSON

LifeWorks Magazine Real Life Award
Parents Magazine Parents' Pick Award
Kids Learn America
Bringing Geography
to Life with People,
Places & History
BY PATRICIA GORDON
& REED C. SNOW

Hands Around the World
365 Creative Ways to
Build Cultural Awareness
& Global Respect
BY SUSAN MILORD

Using Color in Your Art
Choosing Colors for
Impact & Pizzazz
BY SANDI HENRY

Wordplay Café
Cool Codes, Priceless Puzzles
& Phantastic Phonetic Phun
BY MICHAEL KLINE

Kids Care!
75 Ways to Make a Difference
for People, Animals & the
Environment
BY REBECCA OLIEN

Kids Can!® is a registered trademark of Ideals Publications.

Visit Our Website!

To see what's new with Williamson Books and Ideals Publications and learn more about specific titles, visit our website at: www.idealsbooks.com.

To Order Books:

You'll find Williamson Books at your favorite bookstore, or you can order directly from Ideals Publications. We accept Visa and MasterCard (please include the number and expiration date).

Order on our secure website: www.idealsbooks.com

Toll-free phone orders with credit cards: 1-800-586-2572

Toll-free fax orders: 1-888-815-2759

Or send a check with your order to:
Ideals Publications
Williamson Books Orders
2636 Elm Hill Pike, Suite 120
Nashville, Tennessee 37214

Catalog request: web, mail, or phone

Please add **$4.00** for postage for one book plus **$1.00** for each additional book. Satisfaction is guaranteed or full refund without questions or quibbles.